WHO SPEAKS FOR THE BLACK VOTE IN THE AGE OF TRUMP?

The Black Vote Photo – Two ladies, Lillian Baldwin and Kimberley Hanserd of Detroit, Michigan, say "Get Your Knee Off Our Necks!"

The Black Vote Photo – "Excellence." Twice!

The Black Vote Photo – "Congress must Act to Protect the Vote!"

The Black Vote Photo – “Trans, Queer, Poor, Young, Old – All Black Lives Matter” and “Put down Your Shields and Stand with Us. Help us Change the System. No Justice, No Peace.”

The Black Vote Photo – “They have **STOLEN** more than we could ever **LOOT**” and “Justice for Breonna Taylor” – “Black Lives Matter.”

WHO SPEAKS FOR THE BLACK VOTE IN THE AGE OF TRUMP?

WHO SPEAKS FOR THE BLACK VOTE IN THE AGE OF TRUMP?

FREDERICK MONDERSON

SUMON PUBLISHERS

The Black Vote Photo – "Equality makes America Great!"

The Black Vote Photo – "Everybody wanna be **BLACK** until it's time to be **BLACK**!" and "Get in Good Trouble, Necessary Trouble! Vote"

WHO SPEAKS FOR THE BLACK VOTE
IN THE AGE OF TRUMP?

The Black Vote Photo – "Don't Boo, Vote!"

The Black Vote Photo. At the "Tribute to Prof. George Simmonds" at the Victoria 5 Theater in Harlem, "Young" Fred Monderson sat at the feet of his heroes, Dr. Ben-Jochannan and with Prof. George Simmonds in full-chiefly regalia, among others.

ISBN – 978-1-61023-069-8
LCCN - 2020910674

The Black Vote Photo – "Black Lives Matter"

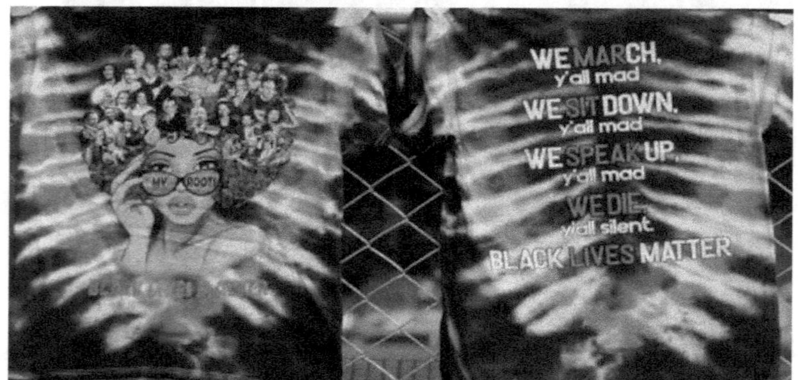

The Black Vote Photo – "Roots and Y'All!"

The Black Vote Photo – Biden President 2020

WHO SPEAKS FOR THE BLACK VOTE IN THE AGE OF TRUMP?

The Black Vote Photo – "Obama, King, Lewis, Sharpton and many great Black-Americans."

The Black Vote Photo – "Black Lives Matter" showcases great Black-Americans and *National Geographic Magazine* having its say.

FREDERICK MONDERSON

TABLE OF CONTENTS

The Black Vote Photo – "Good Trouble, Go Vote!" "Make Necessary Trouble and fight to Vote!"

The Black Vote Photo – "Biden/Harris 2020" "**Vote – Biden – Harris 2020**."

WHO SPEAKS FOR THE BLACK VOTE IN THE AGE OF TRUMP?

The Black Vote Photo – "Ancestor Clear-sightedness, Creativity, Empathy, Courage, Wisdom, Fortitude and Inspiration!"

The Black Vote Photo – “**Vote and Vote**” – “What We Are Asking for Is – Is Simple – **Stop Killing Us**.”

“It is my belief that we need Joe Biden now more than ever before.” **John Lewis**

The Black Vote Photo – “I LOVE BLACK PEOPLE” and **“BLACK LIVES MATTER!”**

“The civil rights movement was based on faith. Many of us who were participants in this movement saw our involvement as an extension of our faith. We saw ourselves doing the work of the Almighty. Segregation and racial discrimination were not in

keeping with our faith, so we had to do something."
John Lewis

The Black Vote Photo – Many who came for the "March of Commitment" and "Stolen Land – Stolen People' playing out in Washington, DC.

1. "GET YOUR KNEE OFF OUR NECKS" BY DR. FRED MONDERSON

In his **Eulogy** for **George Floyd**, Rev. Al Sharpton, in agreement with Martin Luther King III, proposed an August 28, 2020 "March on Washington," a date on the 57th Anniversary of the original March in which Martin Luther King, Jr. gave his "I have a Dream" speech. A principal theme of the march this time was passage of the **John Lewis Voting Rights Act**, an **Extension of the 1965 Voting Rights Act**, as a means of honoring the passing of the last person to speak at the historic 1963 March. In addition, on the 50th Anniversary of that historic gathering in 2013,

President Barack Obama presented Mr. Lewis with the nation's highest honor, the **Medal of Freedom**, for a life committed to achieving much of the American ideal moving towards "a more Perfect Union," this principally is the right to vote.

The Black Vote Photo. "In the Age of Information, Ignorance is a choice" – "A System cannot fail those it was never meant to protect." WEB DuBois - BLM

The Black Vote Photo – "There comes a time when Silence is Betrayal" and "I won't be Quiet so you can be Comfortable."

The Black Vote Photo – Say Their Names!

THE #SAYTHEIRNAMESMEMORIAL
RECOGNIZES 216 BLACK LIVES WRONGFULLY
TAKEN BY BRUTALITY, INJUSTICE & RACISM.
PLEASE HELP US SPREAD AWARENESS &
HONOR THE LIVES OF THOSE TAKEN
TOO SOON. FEEL FREE TO ADD NAMES,
PHOTOS & FLOWERS TO HONOR THOSE WHO
AREN'T REPRESENTED HERE. THIS IS A
LIVING MEMORIAL THAT WILL BE UP
UNTIL THE WEEK OF SEPT 7TH. ♡

PLEASE KNOW EVERYTHING HAS TO BE
REMOVED BY SEPT 10, 2020 - SO PLEASE
COME BACK FOR ANY ITEMS YOU LEAVE
& WANT TO KEEP. OTHERWISE THEY WILL
BE REMOVED.

PEACE ☮ LOVE ♡ COMMUNITY

The Black Vote Photo – Say their Names!

The Black Vote Photo – Marchers on the way to the Lincoln Memorial for "**Commitment**!"

The Black Vote Photo – "A man who stands for nothing will fall for anything." **Malcolm X**

WHO SPEAKS FOR THE BLACK VOTE IN THE AGE OF TRUMP?

SAY THEIR NAMES!

The Black Vote Photo – Say their Names – Aaron Campbell and Abdirahman Salad.

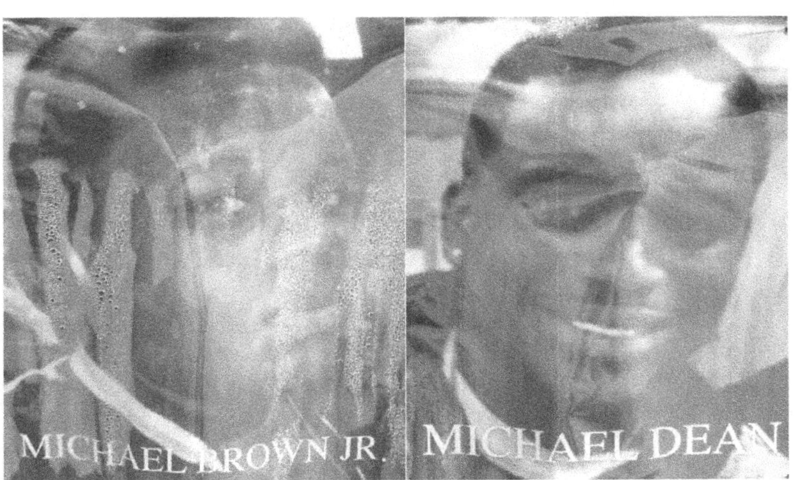

The Black Vote Photo – Say their Names – Michael Brown and Michael Dean.

The Black Vote Photo – "Request a Mail-In Petition at DecrimNatureDC.org – Sign the Petition" "We Can't Breathe!"

The Black Vote Photo – "Love Thy Neighbor, **NO EXCEPTIONS**" – "Black lives Matter."

In addition to the John Lewis measure, the **George Floyd Police Brutality** legislation and pervasive racism in government, institutions and among regular citizens, as well as promulgated divisiveness, across the country even the gross injustice now standard practices, were motivating factors that galvanized the gathering at the historic Abraham Lincoln Memorial on August 20, 2020.

Arriving at the marble steps of the **Lincoln Memorial** and as the crowd filled in on both sides of the **Reflecting Pool**, many listened in approval as speaker after speaker compared the burning issues of 1963 with those of equal magnitude today. However, one such speaker queried, "Why should we be fighting for the same issues Martin Luther King fought for some 57years ago?" While later another marcher queried about the "Numbers" and he then offered "400,000 to 500,000." This seems evident as both sides on the lengthy **Reflecting Pool** were jampacked with many seated on the lawn as others stood near the Podium to hear the message. As penetrating ideas resounded from the Podium, marchers principally chanted in response, time and time again, to calls of "Vote," "Vote Him Out," and need for "Equal Access to the Ballot Box" as well as "Vote for The Black Woman," and "We Must Be United" all the while emphasizing "Black Live Matter!"

Imagine the many voicers rising in ongoing expressions of: "When is Enough Enough;" "We demand Economic Equality;" "Justice and Freedom for All;" "We need Justice;" "No Justice, No Peace;" "Know Justice, Know Peace;" "You say get back, we say fight back;" "The Urgency of Now;" "I Can't Breathe;" "Vote to Get Him Out;" "The road ahead may be difficult, but if we work together we can conquer anything;" "Can we do this Together;" "I'm No Ways Tired;" "We Stand on the shoulders of Giants, but we must now Get Off and Lead;" "Every single person deserves Equality;" "There must be Universal Voting Rights." "Vote as we have never Voted Before.

Significantly, an article published in *The Washington Post* article "We are Sick," for Sunday August 30, 2020, p. 6 by Jessica Contrera, Justin George, Peter Jamison and George Woodson Cox, and being near the podium, they easily recorded a statement of the President of the **National Action Network**, Rev. Al Sharpton. "For too long, you acted like we didn't matter;" Sharpton declared from the steps of the Lincoln Memorial, directly addressing the country. "They say, 'Well, everybody matters.' But everybody hasn't mattered the same in America. The reason we had and we still have to say 'Black Lives Matter' is because we get less health care, like we don't matter. We go to jail longer for the same crimes, like we don't matter … Black lives matter, and we won't stop until it matters to everybody."

Marc Morial, President of **National Urban League**, first thanked Rev. Al Sharpton for organizing this historic march and emphasized, in 1963 those marchers came for Justice and today "We're here for the Right to Vote!" He reminded and more particularly pointed out, the purpose of this March was to seek 'Transference of the Criminal Justice System;' expressing 'the need for a living wage;' seeking 'an end to racism,' the need for 'a proper education for all of children;' but most important he insisted, 'these issues are not negotiable in 2020.' "There must be reform of the police, jobs for youth, and an end to black on black violence." "The people must stand up for the right to vote; we demand passage of the George Floyd Police Brutality Legislation; and Extension of the John Lewis Voting Rights Act. We must not let them suppress our vote."

With equal fervor, Martin Luther King III of **Global Human Right Movement**, spoke of "dismantling systemic racism once and for all," while Shirley Wagner, 71 years old who flew in from Austin Texas, spoke of: "… ones that have gone on and paved the way for us – Martin Luther King Jr. and John Lewis – but my generation hasn't come that far. But I believe in this younger generation; oh, yes, I do. I just know that the young people are going to take us where we need to be" as she pointed to a reporter's phone – "with all that high-tech stuff."

Equally important, as speaker after speaker implored, **SAY THEIR NAMES**, and the mothers of police killings and other violence tell of their woes, the gathering responded to martyrs Breonna Taylor, George Floyd, Jacob Blake, Eric Garner, Trayvon Martin, Ahmaud Arbery, Tamar Rice and many more. In another article, "Familiar old cries are heard in new movement for justice" in *The Washington Post*, Sunday August 30, 2020, p. 7, Paul Duggan, Justin George, Michelle Boorstein and Sydney Trent recounted the experience of many elders who were of Dr. King's time. These remembered, "Separate water fountains, Back of the bus; Colored side of the diner; and No Voting without intimidation." In such pointed reflection, Clifton Price Jr., gave the reason for being on the march as he recounted, "I decided that on my way out of this life, I can contribute to the people I'll leave behind. … It's like the police say: 'I have means, opportunity and motive."

Having experienced and can speak of Emmett Till's agony, he stated further: "When I was a kid, racism was on top of the table, all right? … down through the years, because of laws and demonstrations like this, they can't do that to us out in the open anymore. But the problem hasn't been removed from the system – It's not on top of the table now – it's under the table. It's still there."

The Black Vote Photo – "One Person can make a Difference, and Everyone should Try" (John Kennedy) and "Working-Class Queers."

The Black Vote Photo – Part of the Crowd beside the **Reflecting Pool** enjoying the view and listening to speakers at the Lincoln Memorial Podium.

The Black Vote Photo – Say their Names – Abdoulaye Thiam and Abram Onkgopotse Tiro.

The Black Vote Photo – Say their Names – Michalle Cusseaux and Michelle Lee Shirley.

The Black Vote Photo – Young People at the "March on Washington" "Black Women," "Justice for Breonna," "Black Lives Matter!"

All this notwithstanding, throughout the people kept filling the air with chants of, "You have to protect the Vote;" "From Me to We;" "We will get your knee off our Necks;" "No Justice, No Peace;" "Non Violence doesn't mean Passive Acceptance; it means non-violent Resistance." They kept repeating the names of Eric Garner, George Floyd, Breonna Taylor, Ahmaud Arbery, Brooks, Jacob Blake, Trayvon Martin, Michael Brown, Tamir Rice, and many more particularly as they exited the Martin Luther King, Jr., Memorial shouting "No Justice, No Peace," "I Can't Breathe," "Momma, I Can't Breathe," "Say her Name;" "Say their Names."

Later, a TV personality, Chiney Ogwumike, commenting on experiencing atrocities in real time and observing responses of players of the National Basketball Association (NBA) that influenced similar actions by other athletes, reminded: "This is not about Black people. This is a human problem and we must come together and do something." It was equally mentioned, Michelle Obama confessed to being "Exhausted" by events that were "opening eyes, rattling consciences." Many felt, Black Americans are being bullied, oppressed, depressed and most important, killed in our own country, even though the state deploys Black men in the military to protect this country.

The actions of athletes, in a long line of such protesters, flies in the face of the many who trump, "Shut up and dribble," because you are paid great sums to be entertainers. Jared Kushner spoke of these players being wealthy and "Can take a day off!" No, they affirmed, we recognize the power we possess! We will voice our opposition to unconscionable behaviors to our brothers and sisters and most important, you need to know: "Our bodies are not here for your entertainment." The **Atlanta Hawks** Head Coach, Lloyd Price stated a devastating fact: "I was born black, I'm going to die black, but I don't want to die because I'm black." In honor of home town Atlanta Heroes, C.T. Vivian, Joseph Lowery, John Lewis, Mr. Price helped negotiate opening the State Farm Arena, home of the Hawks, to encourage voting in wake of Carona-virus pandemic and some 10 other arenas have followed suit given Voter Suppression has closed many polling places. Mr. Price further commented on kneeling by NBA and WNBA players which is not a distraction, but a focus on what's happening. It raises awareness to bring about change in form of policy and legislative action. More to come!

The Black Vote Photo – "George Floyd" and "Harriet Escaped, So Rosa Could Sit, and Kamala Could Run!"

"We must never ever give-up. We must be brave, bold and courageous." **John Lewis**

"If you're not hopeful and optimistic, then you just give up. You have to take the long hard look and just believe that if you're consistent, you will succeed." **John Lewis**

2. VALUE OF THE BLACK VOTE BY DR. FRED MONDERSON

The blood of Black martyrs have been shed to defend the nation's territorial integrity through military service, to uphold the constitutional order to bring about the aspirations of a more perfect union, to ensure the guarantees of political expression remain viable, to imbue the nation with sincere religious and spiritual tenacity and to affirm ethical and moral values of the American system but equally the need to expose the ugly sore of American injustice with the scab peeled back, exposing the puss of racism, racial discrimination, degradation and destruction of people, the system itself, and inhumanity of man to man, all infecting and affecting values long cherished, even under camouflage as false prophets as Donald Trump spout under an equally false banner of Make America Great Again, **MAGA**. This is a disguised commercial venture that confuses many believers in a disguised false narrative in conflict with American sayings, ideals, principles and practices. Many of these viewed as cultists, perhaps unknowingly, undermine values and viability of this nation. Their actions, by extension, threaten the very fabric and fiber of the Black experience generating shibboleths as "Vote like never before," especially in the upcoming national election in order to remove the negative influences of Donald Trump and his minions in and out of Congress. It is not far-fetched to think Republicans in the Senate high-five each other as young voters, black and white, seem to count pimples on Biden's face while ignoring the ugly pus oozing from the lips of racists in the White House in conjunction with false narratives echoed by Republican enablers and right-wing media.

While we affirm the **Declaration of Independence's** recognition "All men are created equal" and that, the **Constitution**, "a living document" that extolls the rule of law, these pillars of government are consistently challenged by the Trump administration's consistent efforts that continue to undermine their meanings, values and viability. Many have argued, the functionality of the American system is the last hope for humanity given this is the exuberant expectation as the world, in confronting whatever the malady, viz., pandemic, terrorist attack, domestic mass shootings, hurricanes and other destructive acts of nature, such persons look to America to provide answers, a sympathetic hearing and creative responses, particularly artistic and scientific. When anyone examines a clip depicting gatherings against Barack Obama as President, exhibiting the tremendous frenzy in what came to be represented as Trump's base in his interaction with his false narrative all underscored in the last four years of evidence, even Martians would seem to wonder whether America has descended with him into Mr. Trump's "Shithole" pit.

The Black Vote Photo – "**Invictus** – Manhood Scholarship Perseverance Uplift" and "Say their **Names** at the "March on Washington, 2020."

The Black Vote Photo – Part of the Crowd beside the **Reflecting Pool** and before the Lincoln Memorial with the Washington Monument in rear. "Quality for All" and "Black Lives Matter."

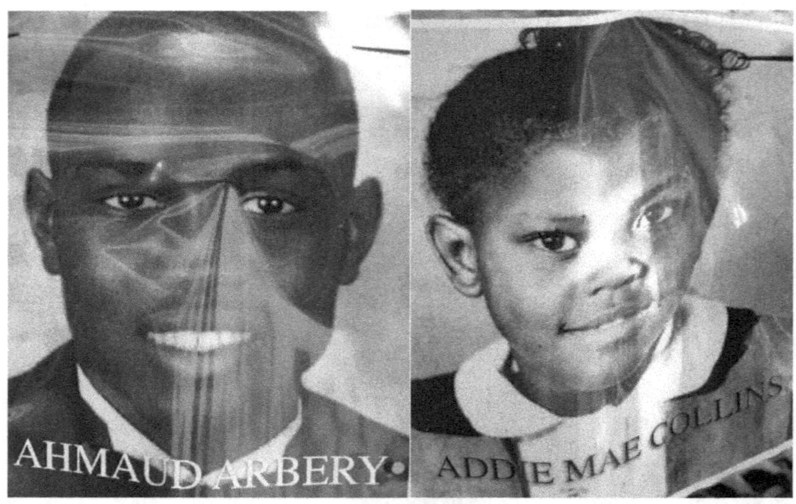

The Black Vote Photo – Say their Names – Ahmaud Arbery and Addie Mae Collins.

WHO SPEAKS FOR THE BLACK VOTE IN THE AGE OF TRUMP?

The Black Vote Photo – Say their Names –Mi'Chance Dunlap Gittens and Morgan London Rankins.

The Black Vote Photo – "No Justice, No Peace" – "Black Lives Matter" and "I Can't Breathe" – # "Justice for George Floyd."

The Black Vote Photo – "Black Lives Matter" in a most conspicuous place beside the "Cross."

The Black Vote Photo – "The Black Panther" and "**How many weren't filmed**?"

WHO SPEAKS FOR THE BLACK VOTE IN THE AGE OF TRUMP?

The Black Vote Photo – No Justice, No Peace – "Warrior Woman" says: **"RESPECT** My **Existence** or **Expect** My **RESISTANCE**." Touché! "Black Lives Matter!"

Today, as the nation is in upheaval resulting particularly from tipping point issues as the murder of George Floyd and the turn to "statues," Prof. Tim Naftali offered a wonderful caveat for thought. This presidential historian suggested, though some leaders of the past have had demonstrated problems of race, their contributions to the nation have been such that these must be preserved. However, it's important that the nation is debating the true nature of the issues whether they be voting, voting suppression, racism, criminal justice, health care, and a whole lot more, must remain front-burner issues. This much in his tool box with more to come, Donald Trump has squandered his opportunity to lead this nation and many believe it's time for a change. So, voters, especially the Black voter, should not be distracted by false narratives. Only a vote for Joe Biden can address the madness, stop the slide and **Build Back Better**.

These days **Social Media**, especially, faces challenges posed in false and confused messages even as the nation approaches the 2020 Presidential election. As such, potential voters need to educate themselves or look to persons who know and understand what's at stake; who the players are, and the intention of their actions. A great deal of ink has been spilt on Russian and other forms of interference in the 2016 election whereby social media was a principal culprit enabling false information to influence voter decisions. The results saw the election of Donald J. Trump given his opponent Hillary Clinton was characterized as possessing a great deal of baggage, political and otherwise.

Important nonetheless, and given the opportunity to serve as President, Mr. Trump said and did much as history records but one telling thing out of many was his statement, "By the time of the 2020 Presidential Election 96 percent of African-Americans will vote for me." Naturally, Mr. Trump has been tagged for making outrageous statements but he's not the only one living in that alternative universe, where he has acolytes serving him without question in that realm of despair posing desperate questions and false fixes.

A recent Social media report revealed, "Mr. Trump is polling at 41 percent among African-Americans." Given the terms "alternate reality" and "alternative facts," and other such terms coined both by Kellyanne and Kayleigh, these numbers are "Trump baby-like" overblown and full of air. Donald Trump has a sordid history of falsity, poor leadership, lying, abuse of anyone who chooses not to see the world from his twisted viewpoint, not to discount use of hollow threats against America's allies while he offers candy for the nation's adversaries. He lacks ethical qualities, demonstrates poor leadership, encourages racist behaviors, is devoid of ethics, empathy and compassion even refuses to accept responsibility for anything that does not match-up to his standard of what seems right by his concept of winning while he rejects anything or anyone who challenges him or makes him look less than presidential, which he is. When Bob Woodward asked him about empathy for Black-Americans he essentially responded, "I did not drink the cool-aid. More important, and undergirding such thoughts, Mr.

Trump has consistently demonstrated behaviors many characterize as racist from his pursuit of what became known as the "Birther Movement" in which he generated a great deal of animosity towards the first African-American President, Barack Obama; who was; nevertheless, well-liked before, during and after his presidency. **From that time on, Trump has confused, divided and employed effort to diminish the effectiveness of the Black vote**. This has been called Voter Suppression. Significantly, even while Blacks analyze and pontificate on whether to vote, persons are working incessantly to subject them to permanent irrelevance. Add this to Trump's attacks on Mexicans, Islam, the Federal Judge, Black lawmakers, especially the four women he told go "go back where you came from," even as all were American citizens, there were born here. Even much more and so the picture becomes clearer why **TRUMP MUST GO**! Therefore, the only option to stop him is a vote for Joe Biden. Let's not forget that great American Icon and Titan, John Lewis's last admonition, "It is my belief that we need Joe Biden now more than ever before."

WHO SPEAKS FOR THE BLACK VOTE IN THE AGE OF TRUMP?

The Black Vote Photo – "**No time** for **Neutrality** – **BLM**;" "A racist system inevitably destroys human beings; it Brutalizes and Dehumanizes Blacks and Whites alike." Kenneth Clark

The Black Vote Photo – Say their Names – Akai Gurley and Alexa Christian.

The Black Vote Photo – Say their Names –Muhlaysia Booker and Mulugea Seraw.

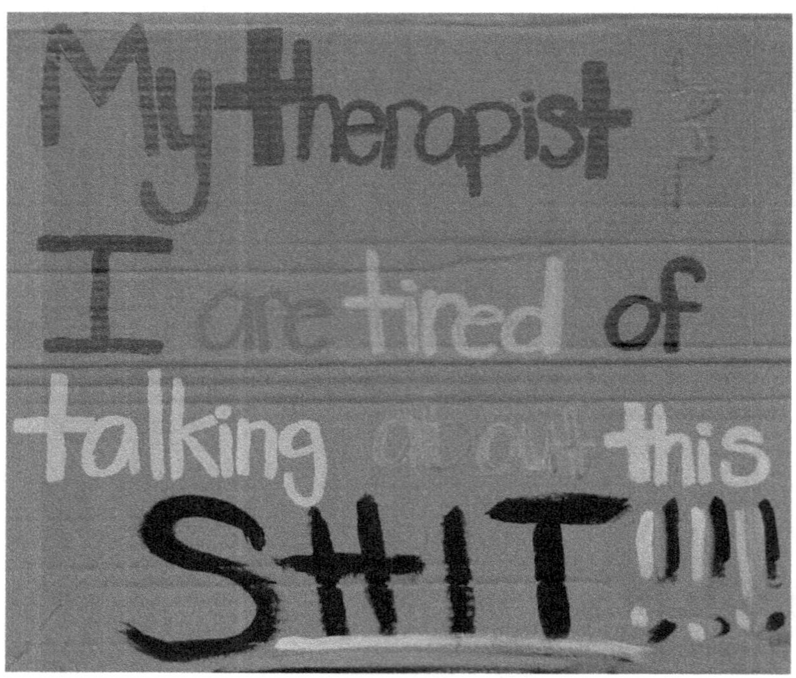

The Black Vote Photo – "My Therapist and I are tired of talking about this **Shit**!!!"

To exacerbate this continuously unfolding reality, a whole litany of other acts include pandering to white supremacist elements even using the department of Justice to undermine the rule of law as he pursues vendettas, against "enemies," perceived and otherwise. He condemns groups as Black Lives matter and Antifa, encourage his supporters to take to the streets to "Liberate," stoking fear the Suburbs will be destroyed. Similarly, in 2018 he pushed the Caravan" as invaders and there's no end to his pathology. He has been accused of trampling on the United States Constitution and has hardly delivered any meaningful foreign policy successes. His behavior towards allies has been dismal while America's traditional enemies seem to have flourished because Mr. Trump has given them a pass or not taken a stance against their outrageous behaviors. In the strange story of Donald J. Trump, "He never made a mistake. He is a persona not a person."

Donald Trump likes to boast he has done more for African-Americans than anyone else. The many assaults he has unleashed on African-Americans outweigh the few jobs he has provided for Blacks, much of which were in service industries and these evaporated in the pandemic. He equally touts money provided for Black Colleges and Universities which has traditionally been part of the national budget. Let's not be confused, some 80 percent of the nation's budget is outside the purview of the president. However, his great misunderstanding has been to underestimate and sell-short the moral fiber that permeates the soul of the African people; their concepts of right and wrong; survival strategies while swimming alongside even against sharks, barracudas and piranhas. Therefore, and realistically, Blacks have traditionally struggled to survive and prosper, for the most part, without the help of the Trumps, even the government. This is clearly exemplified in face of unspeakable horrors throughout a system of slavery, the inhumanity of post-slavery terrorism, share-crop peonage, widespread lynchings, disfranchisement, even murder of significant Black heroes, judicial and extra-judicial killings, particularly of African-Americans over long periods of time as they have sought to maintain and try to meaningfully express the ballot.

The Black Vote Photo – "The Whole Damn System is Guilty as Hell" - "Black Progress Leads to White Outrage!"

Nonetheless, the African-American progeny and community has borne those tragedies with a dignity that distinguishes them from the barbarian perpetrators of the never-ending injustice. Throughout it all Africans expressed forgiveness rather than be burdened by seeming second class citizenship and shackles of hate as espoused by hate-mongers tremendously unaware of their own pathology and dismal history. This is what separates the civilized Africans from the barbarian whose thoughts and actions are not simply uncivilized but cloaked within unconscionable bias, seemingly acting with child-like innocence; yet, expressing hatred in its most vile and deadly mannerism.

As such, those as Donald Trump who actually exist in an alternative universe can utter untold thousands of lies and false statements; yet, seem unable to see such as it relates to true reality. He certainly lied about being concerned about Blacks, doing more than anyone but "Didn't drink the Cool-Aid!"

That is why, in underestimating the moral, ethical, even religious and spiritual underpinnings that constitute the essence of being African, such a mindset dictates opposition to the evil Trump represents and so the belief in any significant percentage of right-thinking Africans will vote for him, is utterly false. Fact is, the African is the necessary political ingredient to end the lies, the reign of terror, incivility, hatred, that President Trump represents. The division and fear he has created. For, as Malcolm X consistently reminded, "The nation is so evenly divided and the Black vote is so crucial, it determines 'who goes to the White House and who goes to the dog-house.'" That is, whether Blacks choose to vote or not, their participation can influence end results. To quote Representative James Clyburn, 2020 is another of those "consequential elections" and Black voters must vote in record numbers against the lies, division, poor leadership, racism, un-American behavior Donald Trump's captivity of the Presidency represents because the soul of the nation is in peril. This time around, the best projectile against Trump is Biden and we must not confuse the issue nor lose the opportunity. Simply viewing who stands behind both Trump and Biden and the impact they can have is an indication of who gets what. Trump has definitely failed in his responsibility and both Black-Americans and the nation may not survive a second term.

The Black Vote Photo – "Silence is Betrayal" – Black Lives Matter" and "Beautiful Black Love."

WHO SPEAKS FOR THE BLACK VOTE IN THE AGE OF TRUMP?

The Black Vote Photo – Say their Names – Alteria Wool amd Alton Sterling.

The Black Vote Photo – Say their Names – Mya Hall and Myra Thompson.

The Black Vote Photo – "I was Afraid to be Here, So Here I Am # **BLM**" - "I Can't Breathe and "Black Lives Matter."

"Do not get lost in a sea of despair. Be hopeful, be optimistic. Our struggle is not the struggle of a day, a week, a month, or a year, it is the struggle of a lifetime. Never, ever, be afraid to make some noise and get in 'trouble,' 'good trouble,' 'necessary trouble.'" John Lewis

"I know Joe Biden as a man of character and dignity – a man who cannot and will not rest when he sees injustice in our American home." **John Lewis**

3. WHO SPEAKS FOR THE BLACK VOTE? BY DR. FRED MONDERSON

Much ado has been uttered saying nothing about how and for whom Black people should vote, particularly in national but also in state and local elections. Given prevailing circumstances, this 2020 presidential election looms larger than most and as such can be classed as "Consequential." Who, therefore do Black voters look to for guidance on how best to fully and constructively leverage that tremendously significant privilege, the right to vote in an American election? As such, specifically for the layman if not for "activist political junkies," knowledge of the political process of voting and thereby pros and cons can help explain what is the significance of that vote. As one Professor pointedly advised, "Let's begin at the beginning." Never mind the ante-bellum or before the Civil War period, but following the **Emancipation Proclamation** (1863), the **Civil War Amendments**, viz., 13th freed the enslaved Africans; 14th gave citizenship to all persons born in the United States; 15th gave the right to vote to all males, native and naturalized citizens.

The period at Civil War's end (1865-1877), **Reconstruction**, represented an attempt to repair the fractured state of the nation to readjust the society after the pain and displacement resulting from the conflict. Much of this occurred in southern lands. One significant difference emerged, that being, the newly freed Black now had the power to register and vote, thereby electing representatives to local, state and national legislative bodies from and in the South where their numbers were significant. That meant, especially, they began to impact the society through rewriting state Constitutions in the new pattern of lawmaking. Unfortunately, however, racism reared its ugly head as whites felt tremendously resentful that former slaves were telling them what to do with force of law backing them. Thus, racism and racist actions escalated playing a significant role in reclaiming power, to again restructure the South to reinstitute "Southern cultural Supremacy" shattered by the war. A number of strategies were therefore implemented to achieve this aim.

The first of the was disfranchisement, a movement designed to effectively block the Black from using political power. "Everyone was in the loop." That is, removing names from voting rolls, use of literary tests, need to pay and show paid poll taxes, intimidation, threats and ultimately lynching either to force Blacks to not vote or flee in forced migration from the places or states they were born into. Racist societies and movements as the Ku Klux Klan, Knights of the White Camelia and several such terror groups emerged, threatening to uphold white values and privileges and intimidating Blacks to that end. As such, systematic and concerted efforts removed hundreds of thousands of Black voters from the voting rolls and similarly from the South even into Northern and Western states. Some whites were removed from voting rolls but Blacks were disproportionately the affected victims.

Through all the tribulations and turmoil to sustain American political ideals of expressing the right to exercise the ballot, Blacks remained loyal to the "Party of Lincoln," for he had issued the **Emancipation Proclamation** and "Radical Republicans" oversaw enactment of the Civil War Amendments they passed. Lincoln's party seemed connected with the movement for right and human dignity. However, this concern over the unfolding plight of Blacks waned leading to the end of Reconstruction and the changing actions many classed as 19th Century terrorism against African-Americans became the order of the day. Still, through this period of "Jim Crow" and "Separate but Equal" legislation undergirding "de facto" and "de jure" racism the face and ideals of the nation changed. In fact, some deemed the 1896 *Plessy v. Ferguson* Supreme Court ruling rather "Separate but Unequal," really "Separate and Unequal," Still, Blacks remained loyal to the Republican Party even as their numbers dwindled from disfranchisement. However, and similarly as the **Declaration of Independence** affirmed, "After a long train of abuse," Blacks abandoned the Republicans and accepted the Democrat Franklin D. Roosevelt's promise of "a New Deal," even though this simply became "the lesser of two evils." However, despite such support for the Democratic Party in 1932, 1936 and again in 1940, it took Asa Philip Randolph's threat to "**March on Washington**" in 1941 on the eve of World War II that forced President Roosevelt to issue an **Executive Order** permitting Blacks to be hired in the War industry. It nevertheless took some 24 more years amidst an arduous, challenging and bloody yet sustained mobilization of direct action resulting in much suffering and death to bring into reality the **Civil Rights Act of 1964** and the **Voting Right Act of 1965**. A corollary example is cited of a CBS report a few years ago, that indicated there were

"100 unsolved Civil Rights murders" on the FBI books and there were probably more. Never mind the hostility and racist actions of Police Chiefs Bull Connors and Clarke, not to mention the agony of the Edmund Pettus Bridge incident John Lewis experienced, non-violence has been the foundation of civil rights protest movements. Blacks very early realized the killer inclination of whites and in resorting to non-violent protest, achieved more than armed conflict could achieve. They did, however, realize, at times, "You must fight fire with fire!"

The Black Vote Photo – "Destroy Hate" and "Black and Proud."

The Black Vote Photo – Say their Names – Adama Traore and Ramarley Graham.

The Black Vote Photo – Say their Names – Najier Salaam and Nathaniel Harris Pickett.

WHO SPEAKS FOR THE BLACK VOTE IN THE AGE OF TRUMP?

The Black Vote Photo – Part of the Crowd answering the "Call for Commitment" at the "March on Washington" August 28, 2020!

The Black Vote Photo – "Black Lives Matter; "Black Lives Matter;" and "Not Today Colonizer."

For the next 50 years from 1965 to 2015, a whole slew of creative actions in protest saw reactive assassination of African leaders in the persons of Malcolm X, Martin Luther King, Medgar Evers, Fred Hampton, and others. Yet, registration and voting continued to expand bringing into being individuals courting the Black vote as well as unprecedented number of Black elected officials. However, one misunderstanding of the voter not schooled in the art of the possible emerged. One such significant misunderstanding for persons not schooled in these matters of legislative arena combat is manifest that the area is not a calm, cove of tranquil cooperation, but a tempestuous lake of challenge and opposition between interests representing haves and have nots. Still, mobilization and exercise of the vote can bring meaningful results, particularly in times of compromise.

The Black Vote Photo – "Voting Equals Democracy." So, "Vote like you have never voted before" – "My People are Black; My Priorities are Black; and My Politics are Black!" **How do you like them "Apples" DA Daniel Cameron, Hershel Walker, Dr. Benjamin Carson?**

WHO SPEAKS FOR THE BLACK VOTE IN THE AGE OF TRUMP?

The Black Vote Photo – "Your Badge doesn't make you Judge, Jury and Executioner" and with "Liberty and Justice for All."

I'm often reminded of the now departed Congressman Major Owens, who, addressing a forum in Brooklyn, New York, stated: "People often ask why is the Black Caucus in Congress and what does it do?" His response was, "It is not so much the legislation that we, the Black Caucus, create and enact, but what we stop. So much frivolous legislation is proposed in Congress designed to penalize the poor, it is only by being there and forming coalitions and com promise with people of good will and conscience that we can stop it." Therefore, we must register and vote and especially in these challenging times, we must vote in unprecedented numbers. Across the nation whites are almost 100 percent registered and they vote but Blacks far too less so and they must seek to match these totals.

The Black Vote Photo – "No Justice, No Peace!" "Stop all No Knock Warrants;" "Ban All Choke Holds;" "End Racist Justice and Prison System;" "Stop Police Funding" if they don't act right.

We must continuously stay vigilant and work to counter ongoing efforts in the form of voter suppression, a principal of Republicans, seeking to nullify the Black vote. Again, we must never forget, Malcolm X reminded, "The nation is so politically divided," the importance and significance of the Black vote is such, "Blacks can determine who go to the White House and who go to the Dog House!"

The Black Vote Photo – "Can't Colonize the Vibe" – "Obama could have never been elected with 3 Baby Mamas, but Trump can??? "**Black Lies Matter**!"

"There is still work yet to be done." **John Lewis**

"Get out there and push and pull until we **redeem the soul of America**." **John Lewis**

4. WHO SPEAKS FOR THE BLACK VOTE II? BY DR. FRED MONDERSON

If you want a good education you attend a good school with challenging and concerned teachers. If you want to learn a skill you choose a teacher skilled in the art form you're engaged in. When it comes to politics, mobilization, registration and the impact of the vote we need to look to persons with the proper knowledge of this area of social combat. That is, in addition to practitioners of the craft, we look to the experienced hand in government who knows the opposing players, their strategies and tactics and how to counter their actions. For example, the actions of individuals dedicated to disfranchisement, to strife and what are Black demands for equality and justice, etc., falls within their purview of those observers. Naturally, such political warriors must prove worthy of our confidence. So much so, we can come to rely on their insightful experience from their studied observations of the battlefield upon which they operate. John Robert Lewis was a titan in this respect and James Clyburn can be considered the political guru equated with Anthony Fauci of pandemic fame.

Therefore, and while there are state and local actors across the spectrum, one of the most brilliant and sustained, battle-tested political figures who commands great respect is Congressman James Clyburn (D. SC). As a "warrior in the belly of the beast" with a panoramic view of the political landscape, Mr. Clyburn is amply positioned to comprehend the full machinations of the national government's actions, he counts the numbers, observes the manner in which funds are disbursed, and is responsible for much more. As such, we must listen to James Clyburn and the allies he can count on in those critical moments to evaluate and assess pending legislation and effectiveness, who is targeted and whether it's good or bad and what is needed in response, good or bad. Just as important, politicians count the numbers of votes, who votes, where, and providing of course, they "bring home the bacon;" so this becomes a tool in efforts seeking support from such expanding voting or community blocks.

But first, oftentimes a historical context is always important in developing perspective regarding a people's experiences. That perspective can lend weight in assessing contemporary situations when determining courses of action given prevailing conditions. It's often been stated, Blacks often feel there is no need for them to vote for there is no reward if they do. That is not a correct sentiment for a number of reasons.

The Black Vote Photo – "Black Lives Matter" and Colin Kaepernick **HERO** as "7"

WHO SPEAKS FOR THE BLACK VOTE IN THE AGE OF TRUMP?

The Black Vote Photo – Say their Names – Andre Green and Antwon Rose Jr.

The Black Vote Photo – Say their Names – Ollie Brooks and Nina Pop.

The Black Vote Photo – "Veterans Support Black Lives Matter VFW Post 9619" - **The Lincoln Memorial**, site of the 1963 historic "March on Washington" of Dr. Martin Luther King's famed "I have a Dream" speech and now crowds gather to hear the message of this year's "Commitment March" August 28, 2020.

The Black Vote Photo – "We declare our right on this earth to be a man, to be a human being, to be respected as a human being, to be given the right of a human being in this society, on this earth, in this day, which we intend to bring into existence **BY ANY MEANS** necessary" Malcolm X.

WHO SPEAKS FOR THE BLACK VOTE IN THE AGE OF TRUMP?

The Black Vote Photo – "Miss Me yet?" – "Vota Por La Juventos" – "In god We Trust?"

First, it is general practice that politicians and their agents "mine" the voting records to recognize who vote, who register and who do not vote. These voting persons and communities are then focused to get their continued support. Second, voting, like filling out the Census, helps determine which communities get funding for which projects. Third, electing individuals to represent various communities, enables those elected officials to get slices of the budget for social programs, housing starts, educational programs, hospital and health care related matters, transportation upgrade, libraries and much more. More important, however, we cannot overlook the importance of not being represented, either through denial of the vote or failure even more important refusal to participate in the electoral process. However, when persons who are disillusioned for one reason or another, realize the hard, cold facts evident either in the consequences of their non-involvement or some precipitating act, they then come around and become resolute participants.

The Black Vote Photo – “Honor their Memory by Fighting Voter Suppression.”

The Black Vote Photo – “I see you BLM.”

Again, within the historical construct, we look at two scenarios. In *The Essential Writings and Speeches of Martin Luther King*, Jr. Edited by James M. Washington (New York: Harper Collins Publishers,

1991: 564), Dr. King speaks to the question: "Where do we go from here?" Though these figures are "old" or "Civil Rights days" they can yet be applied to today's circumstances:

"Negro registration in almost every southern state has increased by at least 100 percent, and in Virginia and Alabama, by 300 and 600 percent, respectively. There are no illusions among southern segregationists that these gains are important. The old order has already lost ground; its retreats are symbolized by the departure from public life of Sheriffs Clarke and Bull Connor. Far more important, the racists have restructured old parties to cope with the merging challenges. In some states, such as Georgia and Alabama, white supremacy temporarily holds the state house, but it would be a foolish and shortsighted politician who felt secure in this victory. In both of these states the most serious contender in recent elections was with a former governor who publicly welcomed the Negro vote, shaped his policies to it and worked with Negro political organizations in the campaign. This change is itself a revolutionary event. This amazing transformation took place in one decade of struggle after ten decades of virtually total disfranchisement. The future shape of southern politics will never again operate without a strong Negro electorate as a significant force."

"Even in Mississippi, where electoral advances are not yet marked, a different form of change is manifest. When Negroes decided to march for freedom across the state, they boldly advanced to the capital itself in a demonstration of thirty thousand people. Ten years before, a Mississippi Negro would have submissively stepped to the gutter to leave the sidewalk for a white man. Ten years before, to plan a meeting, Negroes would have come together at night in the woods as conspirators. A decade ago, not a single Negro entered the legislative chamber of the South except as a porter or a chauffeur. Today eleven negroes are members of the Georgia House."

Again, in *America in Black and White*: *One Nation, Indivisible – Race in America* by Stephan Thernstrom and Abigail Thernstrom (New York: Simon and Shuster, 1997: 462) in Chapter 16, on **Voting Rights** the authors offers a quote: "Before we had the right to vote, politicians call us niggers," ran a 1981 political advertisement aimed at Black voters in Mobile, Alabana. "After we received the right to vote, but our numbers were few, they called us Nigras. When we reached 5,000, they called us colored. (At) 10,000 they called us black people. Now that we have reached 50,000, they call us Commissioner Wicks, Judge Cain Kennedy, Representative Yvonne Kennedy, and Senator Figures. If you don't want to go back to square one, vote for Mims and Greenough."

So, we see how far voting takes Black people. Today, there are essentially two major political parties, Democrats and Republicans. There is one Black Republican in the Senate and three Black Democrats of 100 Senators and perhaps one Republican in the

House of Representatives of 435 members. There are fifty-three Black Democrats in the House. As stated earlier, in coalition with even 22 white members, the Black Caucus can be a formidable watchdog on frivolous legislation. Today, Republicans, whether through fear of Donald Trump or a true indication of their questionable behaviors, despite the poor praises of Donald Trump by Ben Carson and DA Cameron among others, when Black-Americans face oppression, Republicans remain silent in face of Trump's mayhem, lies, poor leadership, and lack of empathy for Black pain and suffering, as death and injustice mount.

The Black Vote Photo – "Black Lives Matter" "I Can't Breathe; "No Justice – No Peace;" "Where is the Love;" "Just Being Me" and "Racism;" "Police Brutality;" "Murder." "**This is America**!"

The Black Vote Photo – Say their Names – Antwun Shumpert and Aries Clark.

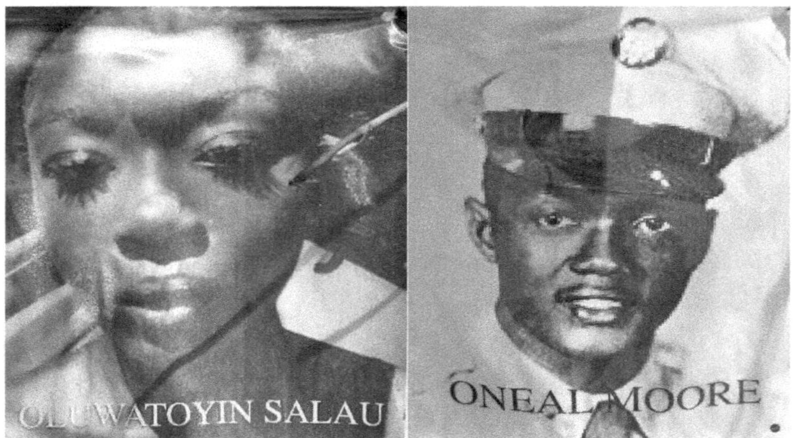

The Black Vote Photo – Say their Names – Oluwatoyin Salau and Oneal Moore.

WHO SPEAKS FOR THE BLACK VOTE IN THE AGE OF TRUMP?

The Black Vote Photo – "Beauty begins the Moment you decide to be Yourself" and "Rep. John Lewis," tireless Champion of **The Right to Vote**.

"**Vote like you have never voted before.**" **John Lewis**

"I remember back in the 1960s - late '50s, really - reading a comic book called "Martin Luther King Jr. and the Montgomery Story.' Fourteen pages. It sold for 10 cents. And this little book inspired me to attend non-violence workshops, to study about Gandhi, about Thoreau, to study Martin Luther King, Jr., to study civil disobedience." **John Lewis**

The Black Vote Photo – Part of the Crowd.

5. WHO SPEAKS FOR THE BLACK VOTE III? BY DR. FRED MONDERSON

Without question Black voting strength has risen dramatically into the new century considering where African-Americans were consigned in the aftermath of systematic disfranchisement following

Reconstruction. In the hundred years after, the struggle had to be systematically waged to achieve the 1964 **Civil Rights Act** and the 1965 **Voting Rights Act** with the latter's provision that the law needs to be renewed every 25 years, for fear it could be weakened through changing times. This was done by the Supreme Court in **Shelby**... in 2013. Nevertheless, Black political strength, sophistication and the strategic planning these options often demonstrate leaves no question those with a full understanding knows what must be done. Still, there are untold numbers, particularly through disappointment and dissatisfaction, who choose not to register and oftentimes refuse to exercise the right to vote, even after registering to vote. Then again, they sometimes listen to the wrong people, and I mean Black figures who pontificate for whatever reason, receive their "0 pieces of silver," and end up essentially leading these people down the path of ineffectiveness, politically speaking. Simply put, politics rule the land and politicians respond to people who vote, period! Therefore, "if you don't vote, you don't count!"

Personally, as someone who voted in every election since 1972, I don't vote for candidates. I vote for me and instruct my young of their obligation to vote. I choose candidates and that's it. I teach my children the value of the vote.

We must seek to understand why Republicans particularly seek to suppress the vote of Black-

Americans. Recently, a young New Yorker submitted a proposal to Congress seeking an "Anti-Voter Suppression Law" that stated in part, "One of the tenets of the legislation must require that the party perpetrating the act of Voter Suppression, be it the illegal purging of voter rolls, the inconvenience of the closing of polling sites, or the delivery of an unbelievable number of inoperable voting machines into specific neighborhoods. No voter in America should have to stand in line for hours to cast a vote, mainly due to the manipulations of either the Republican or the Democratic party. The legislation must, emphatically, require that the candidates running for office, and representing the party utilizing the act of suppression be, totally, disqualified and not allowed to assume the office sought in the election, be it local, state, or federal."

Because there are fewer Republicans than Democrats and Independents make the difference, a consistent part of the Republican political strategy has been suppression of the Black vote while hoping to attract Independents to offset the difference. Even Donald Trump has indicated, essentially, efforts should be made to curtail democratic voting because "When Democrats vote in full strength, Republicans lose." Citizens must seek to understand, voter suppression is an orchestrated phenomenon that is systematically executed from state legislatures down to local party precinct operations. One of the most pressing issues former Attorney General Eric Holder has had to contend with has been Voter Suppression especially across Southern State Houses. Therefore, what emanates from State Houses is put in practice at local levels.

As far back as the age of **Reconstruction**, Southern racists have practiced Voter Suppression and they were successful in the systematic efforts unleashed against the newly Freed African. Somewhere between 1870-1900, millions of voters were disfranchised, scrubbed from Southern voting rolls so that Southern Supremacy would triumph. Back then, racists practiced intimidation by standing in proximity to voting boxes and intimidated Black voters. Some sought to know how they voted through ingenious means then reported this to employers who fired those voting against their wishes or interests. Threats of lynching and lynchings itself were means to intimidate and keep Blacks away from polls. Literacy tests, evidence of paid poll taxes, property taxes and other such requirements were used successfully against the Black Voter. The "Grandfather Clause" was implemented to shield white voters who could not pass the literacy test and this remained in effect until 1915 when the Supreme Court outlawed its practice. Signs were posted to show voters in which direction polling places were located. In most cases these signs pointed in the wrong direction. There were instances when voters arrived at polling stations after a long trek, they were told they had to go to another such place and this was time consuming. Sometimes when they finally arrived the polls were closed. In recent years one elderly Black man was quoted as saying he donned his best outfit and they had him walking in different directions for more than six hours and finally he could not vote.

We must understand, such practices are not ancient or go back to the 19th Century exclusively. As recent as the "age of Barack Obama," post 2008, Republican playbooks were actively misinforming voters. One ridiculous ploy stated essentially, "Republicans vote on day one, and Democrats vote on day two." Others said, "If you had as much as a parking ticket, police would be nearby to arrest you or collect the fine." This had an effect. Even disparaging, sometimes threatening literature was distributed to dissuade potential Democratic voters to stay away from the polls. Seeking to be Mayor of New York City, Rudy Giuliani posted signs in the Black community that read: "Rudy G. fights racism." Yet, he turned out to be the biggest racist New York City ever produced. As such then, voters should educate themselves as to the process. They should look to persons who know.

One such person, this voter always looks to is Representative James Clyburn, but there are others. Mr. Clyburn, is the highest-ranking Black Member of Congress. He is a Democrat who knows all the "ins and outs" of the impact of voting and the strengths and benefits thereto. Remember he told us, "A Black woman on Joe Biden's ticket is a plus, not a must!" This is because it's more important to remove Donald Trump from the White House than to make the choice of a Black woman on the ticket an absolute necessity.

WHO SPEAKS FOR THE BLACK VOTE IN THE AGE OF TRUMP?

The Black Vote Photo – "March on Washington, 2020" and "Black Excellence."

The Black Vote Photo – Say their Names – Alfred Olango and Ashtian Barnes.

The Black Vote Photo – Say their Names – O'Shae Marquis Terry and Pamela Shantay Furnier.

The Black Vote Photo – "Vote for Reform" – "Say Their Names."

"Freedom is not a state; it is an act. It is not some enchanted garden perched high on a distant plateau where we can finally sit down and rest. Freedom is the continuous action we all must take, and each generation must do its part to create an even more fair, more just society." **John Lewis**

"I gave Blood on that Bridge in Selma, Alabama, for the right to vote!" **John Lewis**

6. "OLD PAPI" AND THE BLACK VOTE! BY DR. FRED MONDERSON

Oftentimes, the last battle is not the final one on the homeward march; and thus, soldiers have to turn and do one more because of time and circumstance. Today, in America, that one battle, in fact one war, must be fought. Again, Malcolm X, the "Shining Black Prince" reminded, "History is a good teacher." As such, back in 2012, as President Barack Obama headed into his re-election campaign, a racist mantra emerged entitled, "Old Papi says, Don't Re-Nig!" This powerful statement raised a number of questions, the first of which was, 'How old is Papi?' In this case, historical context is important. But first, **Let's not "Re-Trump!"**

In the Pre-Civil War period, hardly any Blacks had the vote, and if any, very few. We must remember, *Dred Scott v. Sandford* (1857), that "Blacks were not citizens," etc., fell in this category and time. However, the ravages of the Civil War (1860-1865) produced the **Civil War Amendments**, viz., 13th – freed the slaves; 14th granted citizenship to anyone born in America: and 15th granted the right to vote. Naturally, these amendments flew in the face of Chief Justice Roger Taney's ruling that 'Blacks were not citizens, could not bring suit in federal court, and Blacks had no rights which a white person must respect.'

The Radical Republicans who emerged as the dominant legislative force in the immediate Post-Civil War years, produced the three ground breaking amendments, most particular the 15th, concerning the right to vote. The African, now freed from enslavement, rushed to take advantage of the new political freedom and help craft a more just society in wake in the new **Reconstruction** movement.

They were, for the most part, successful electing members to state and local legislatures and sending members to Congress, both in the House and in the Senate. The rapid emergence of Black political power enabled them to be principals in crafting new constitutions and electing members, particularly for southern state houses. However, the now 'prostrate south,' incensed that their former slaves were now 'calling the political shots, resorted to a number of machination strategies to regain white control and power in form of Southern supremacy. The creation of terror mechanisms was a principal development in which Black voters were intimidated to the extent they feared for their lives. The Ku Klux Klan, Red Shirts, Knights of the White Camelia, etc., were actively involved in orchestrating and executing the many facets of 19th Century American terrorism, particularly in lynchings. In addition, social and economic threats were the order of the day as well as seizure of black property, which forced man to flee west or north. As events unfolded, in wake of the "Betrayal of 1876" especially, the **Radical Republicans** suspended their vigorous defense of the Freedman, and the national government remained silent in face of the abuses unfolding all across the South, Blacks yet clung to the Republican Party, because it was "**The Party of Lincoln**," who had ended their bondage.

In all this, the Republican Party ignored the plight of the Freed Africans who were being systematically and maliciously purged from voting rolls in the south at an alarming rate as the Grandfather Clause and Jim Crowism culminated in *Plessy v. Ferguson*, an 1896 Supreme Court ruling that created, **Separate But Equal** which many determined to actually be **Separate and Unequal**. This forceful separation was particularly evident in measured educational resources where for every one dollar spent on a Black Child's education, ten to fifteen dollars was spent on that of a White Child's.

Through Teddy Roosevelt's "Square deal" in 1900, despite the heroic actions of Black soldiers in his "Charge up San Juan Hill" in the Spanish-American War (1900-1902); and the promises of Woodrow Wilson particularly after the role of Black soldiers who went abroad to "Save the World for Democracy" but came home to a dismal reception, many were forced to leave their homes because of racist actions in several forts and towns bordering such facilities. So much so, W.E.B. DuBois reminded and prophetically acclaimed, "We went abroad fighting and we return fighting" against the mounting inequities and terror that gave rise to **The Klansman** and **Birth of a Nation** all wallowed in "Gone with the Wind" mentality and reality. Then, amidst the rising wealth of the roaring twenties, lack of Black progress, the great Depression happened, and Blacks finally proclaimed, "Republicans ain't got our backs!" So, in the 1932 election, Franklin D. Roosevelt promised a "New Deal" to address the rising economic catastrophe and hopefully improve the lot of all Americans. So, Black voters left the Republican Party and voted for the Democratic Party. As such, Blacks voted for the Democrat Franklin Roosevelt in 1932, 1936 and in 1940, then again in 1944, by which time the world was at war though America only entered in 1941.

The nation reached out to Britain and its allies in a "Lend-Lease" program to support their effort and unleashed a revved-up production process that proved to be "the arsenal of democracy." That is, the wherewithal of men, supplies, ships and more that turned the tide in favor of the allies.

The Black Vote Photo – "Black Lives Matter" and "Unapologetically Black and Educated."

The Black Vote Photo – "**Black Power over Africa**" and "Like the Martin Luther King Memorial, it must engulf the World!"

The Black Vote Photo – "Resist" and "Equal Justice Under the Law" – "100% pro-black period – I ain't explaining shit!"

WHO SPEAKS FOR THE BLACK VOTE IN THE AGE OF TRUMP?

The Black Vote Photo – “Black Lives Matter” and “Hero!”

“We are tired. We are tired of being beaten by policemen. We are tired of seeing our people locked-up in jail over and over again.” **John Lewis**

“If you’re not hopeful and optimistic, then you just give up. You have to take the long hard look and just believe that if you’re consistent, you will succeed.” **John Lewis**

7. A CONSEQUENTIAL ELECTION BY DR. FRED MONDERSON

The African-American "Shining Prince" Malcolm X, often held, "History is a good teacher." Today, as we seek to determine what is meant by a "Consequential Election," there are a number of landmark instances along the historical continuum that serve as good examples of this important occurrence. The time periods in which these elections occurred, the resulting social, civic even economic consequences that resulted always served as barometers of future political and election action. As such, and to further help understand elections, we look to the U.S. Census which happens every 10 years and is the basis upon which "redistricting" of Election Districts is done. Generally, the party in government, more often than not, redraw district lines that favor them in the next and hopefully subsequent elections. Oftentimes they go too far and such actions are termed "Gerrymandering." When challenged in the courts, their actions are oftentimes deemed illegal since their skewing of the political landscape is generally designed to suppress the voting strength of a particular group who may vote against the interest of the party in power.

Because elections are a state responsibility, the party with a state legislative majority generally seeks to legislate any number of measures that "cleanse the voting rolls" which in fact is disfranchisement or voter suppression. Recently pushed by Republicans, this strategy in the type of law, has been in the form of requiring state issued identification which slows the registration process when offices are closed, sparse or placed at a distance making it a challenge to get there, especially for the aged and disabled. Most important, the requirement that a state Identification be presented to vote poses a problem, particularly for those who "Can't" get the ID and therefore, in most cases, become ineligible to vote. This is significantly, a form of voter suppression. In addition, some voter registration offices are even closed permanently or have reduced hours, reducing the number of such places in which voter services are facilitated, thereby further reducing the number of registered voters or "cleansing" the rolls. Felony prisoners are often stripped of their right to vote, generally even after they have paid their debt to society. When calamities such as hurricanes, floods, even fires destroy record keeping centers, this sets back the identification process and hinders registration and therefore affects the right to vote. Registrars sometimes make demands for identification of Seniors and the poor which is often difficult to provide. As such, if persons are not vigilant, upgrade and frequently maintain their voting status, they can be easily disfranchising or purged from the voting rolls. Then there are the natural, run-of-the-mill errors, which happens at the Board of Election, whether human or mechanical. These can include mis-filing of names of persons registered, broken machines, otherwise missing or defective registration, and let's not forget, more negative campaigning directed against opponents and all other possible means hopefuls can concoct to get elected, or re-elected. Very often, caught up in the throes of being elected or getting re-elected, politicians or representatives "low key" addressing citizens' concerns and together with election day shenanigans which impacts turnout, these go a long way in determining the consequential nature of an election and final vote tally. Thus, the end result of not being active and vigilantly involved results in what former President Barack Obama expressed regarding the 2016 election, "What if we are wrong," about the projected outcome. Now add to this foreign" or "Russian" interference and so we got Donald Trump.

The Constitution requires federal officers face the voters every two years. That is to say; first, they are 435 Representative Districts across the country creating that number of House of Representative members, or seats. This number is calculated and demarcated after the census based on population size occupying each district. The Census numbers also determine where resources are distributed. Nevertheless, these House of Representative members essentially serve for a two-year period and in this category are, therefore, up for re-election. The Senate is representative of the 50 states with two senators each who serve for a period of 6 years per term. Because of the great responsibility of this deliberative body; more so than the House of Representative which is essentially a "money" or "finance" institution as part of its legislative function; only one third of the Senate faces the electorate every two years. For example, as in case of the upcoming 2018 Mid-Term Election, all 435 House of Representative members were up for re-election but only 33 Senators or so of a regular term and 2 special elections slots for the full six-year term were on the ballot. However, because of contemporary and prevailing societal conditions in the "Age of Trump," as in the mid-term of 2018, this national election of November 2020 becomes **Consequential**. The Office of the President, however, is the principal office up for grabs in 2020 and again every four years. Oftentimes persons run on the President's "Slate" and the outcome is considered the "coat-tail effect." As such, given the current situation, the 2020 election takes on more meaning for control of Congress.

The Black Vote Photo – "End Mass Incarceration" and the "New Jim Crow."

The Black Vote Photo – More of the crowd cooling it and listening to Speakers at the Podium.

The Black Vote Photo – At the Martin Luther King Memorial – "Good and Necessary Trouble," Protect the Vote" and "Melanin Gives you Super Powers!"

The Black Vote Photo – "The iconic Malcolm X – Advocated "**By Any Means Necessary**!"

The Black Vote Photo – "I Know 'Black Lives Matter' – Do You?" "Joe Biden – Kamala Harris 2020" and "Racism is an Illness." So "**Vote**" to be rid of Trump and Racism!

The Black Vote Photo – The people engaged! "Black Lives Matter" – "Stolen Land" – "Stolen People." The People sure are Engaged, expressing their views about the state of society under Trump!

The Black Vote Photo – "Black Lives Matter" and "**Black Power**."

Back in time, Adam Clayton Powell gave a remarkable speech in Harlem, New York, in which he asked, as entitled, "What's in your hand?" There he highlighted Jesus with' "two nails on the cross" and the significance of the 1965 **Voting Rights Act**, which in fact reinforced the 1868 - 15th Amendment to the Constitution giving the vote, essentially, to males born in the U.S. Significantly, these two legislative accomplishments empowered African-Americans through the right to vote. However, nefarious individuals especially, often choose to nullify that entitlement or are generally happy when Blacks refuse to exercise the inherent power such political gains represent. Malcolm X, on the other hand, insightfully recognized how evenly divided or politically balanced Republicans and

Democrats were, and so emphasized the importance of the Black vote which could help determine, "Who goes to the White House and who goes to the dog house." A modern example of this phenomenon was the "Judge Roy Moore for Senate" fiasco in which the race was "close" until; unexpectedly, Blacks threw their weight, their vote, behind the Judge's opponent, and this force of will determined the result, and this is to be expected in similar situations. Again, in the 2020 Democratic Primary Joe Biden's candidacy was way behind until James Clyburn urged Blacks in South Carolina to "**Go Vote Biden**" and the result is history.

Even more significant, given African-Americans have fought unending for America's defense and traveled a long and arduous road to win the vote, register to vote, and struggled to exercise the privilege of the vote; we must, therefore, never lose sight of voting significance. In South Africa people spent hours and hours standing in line to cast the ballot for the first time in the most consequential election of their time brought about by global pressures against Apartheid and the significance of Nelson Mandela's 26-years in prison standing on the principle of the sanctity of one man, one vote!

Perhaps elements of the population in these United States do not understand the inherent power of the vote; how the vote influences the nation's economic, political and moral-social landscape and the true meaning of a consequential election. On the other hand, people with a true sense of history and an understanding of the African-American experience and how difficult it has been to ascend to the mountain-top Barack Obama represented, must now be involved to the political hilt. Sadly, however, within a mere 18-months, gains Mr. Obama struggled to achieve as the nation's first twice-elected African-American President, much has been revoked by Donald Trump; others that "still stand" are threatened and strictures are being put in place that will impact, control and determine the nation's path for the "next 40-years." Donald Trump and Mitch McConnell boast of the nearly 300 "Conservative Judges" they put in place. This must change, especially for the sake and safety of African-Americans. While the cat is away, the mouse will play to win! Nevertheless, traps and glue sticks can keep that mouse in check.

As an example, of the inherent hatred of the Blackman, what else, since he "footballs" Mr. Obama every day, the following are some significant Obama accomplishments Donald Trump has reversed.

1. DACA – Deferred Action for Childhood Arrivals - 2012
2. Stop transfer of surplus Military equipment to local police – 2015
3. Normalizing Relations with Cuba – 2014
4. The Paris Climate Agreement
5. Offshore and Artic Oil Drilling – 2016
6. Net Neutrality – 2015
7. The Clean Water Rule
8. Caps on Greenhouse Gas Emissions at Power Plants

9. Scope of National Monuments
10. Bathroom Protections for Transgender Students
11. NAFTA North America Free Trade Agreement
12. Trans-Pacific Partnership
13. Extension of Fair Housing legislation passed in 1968 and re-authorized in 2015, enabling low cost housing to be built in the Suburbs. Now, Trump has reversed this important provision in a racist dog-whistle, some believe is actually a blow-horn.

Given Donald Trump's unending invoking of the "Cool Ruler's" name, one has to wonder whether it is, "P, Q, R. S, or, I even T" envy.

Nevertheless, torrential outpouring of voting strength can send a clear and convincing message not simply to Mr. Trump but to Republicans and Democrats as well. "Respect the Black vote!" This way, meaningful and respected Black input can help shape the future direction of the nation. Again, we must never relinquish the significance of the vote.

WHO SPEAKS FOR THE BLACK VOTE IN THE AGE OF TRUMP?

The Black Vote Photo – "Get Your Knee Off My Neck" and "Arrest the Cops who Killed Breonna Taylor."

The Black Vote Photo – Say their Names – Askari Roberts and Crystalline Barnes.

The Black Vote Photo – Say their Names – Patrick Kimmons and Paul O'Neal.

The Black Vote Photo – "Capitalism Creates Poverty and Racism" – "Unite Class and Color, Overthrow the 1%."

In January of 2016, Rep. James Clyburn (D. SC) pointed to the consequential nature of the upcoming presidential election. Throughout that year, President Obama strenuously and vigorously expressed such in campaigning for Hillary Clinton. With all her "imperfections" Blacks would have had influence with Hillary! Instead, many followed Sean Combs, "Puff Daddy," "Puffy," "P. Diddy," "Diddy," a confused young man, who insisted Blacks "Hold the Vote." Instead we get Paris Dennard, Mark Burns, Kanye West, DA Cameron, Ben Carson, the Heritage Foundation poster image, all of whom earned their "30 pieces of chitlins," Malcolm X called it "guts." To these we must recognize the sign carried by recently deceased Herman Cain as he sat in company of others without masks in support of the Tulsa Rally. Then there are Black guards who protect Mr. Trump, Black waiters, Black men with mops, no Black millionaires, but significant roll-back of Criminal Justice reforms, with focus on more equitable sentencing, time served and re-entry efforts designed to reduce recidivism. Noticeable is the private prison industry undergoing a tremendous resurgence and Black and Brown people overwhelmingly their tenants behind the profit motive surge.

Nonetheless and much more significant, many still do not realize, the transformation of America Donald Trump is effectuating can practically be viewed especially from the judicial appointments he has put in place. The Internet once reported, "as of July 10, 2018, the United States Senate has confirmed 43 Article III judges nominated by President Trump, including 2 Associate Justice of the Supreme Court of the United States, 22 Judges for the United States Courts of Appeals, 20 Judges for the United States District Courts, and 0 Judges for the United States

Court of International Trade.[2] There are currently 91 nominations to Article III courts awaiting Senate action, including 1 for the Supreme Court, 12 for the Courts of Appeals, 76 for the District Courts, and 2 for the Court of International Trade.[3] [At that time] There were (currently) [1 vacancy] on the Supreme Court, 14 vacancies on the U.S. Courts of Appeals, 129 vacancies on the U.S. District Courts, 2 vacancies on the U.S. Court of International Trade,[3] and 31 announced federal judicial vacancies that will occur before the end of Trump's first term (1 for the Supreme Court, 7 for the Courts of Appeals, and 22 for District Courts). [4] Trump has not made any recess appointments to the federal courts."

As we look to the future, African people must never forget African-American blood, sacrifice and tears that soaked and fertilized the wealth of this American land; and most important, they must also realize, "there are no permanent enemies only permanent interests." Our ancestors were oftentimes worked to death, unpaid and penniless under cruel and inhumane conditions; our men, women and children were brutalized, disrespected, killed and abused, as we faced racism, discrimination and terrorism responsible for nearly 4040 lynchings from 1870-1950, these must not be forgotten. There's been no accounting for this tragedy and none held accountable as the government turned a blind eye toward our plight. Still, like Mother Emanuel Saints, these martyrs forgave the "dirty, Rotten Scoundrels."

WHO SPEAKS FOR THE BLACK VOTE IN THE AGE OF TRUMP?

The Black Vote Photo – "I Can't Breathe" and "What does the Lord require?"

The Black Vote Photo – "White Silence = Consent" and Black Lives Matter" now more!

The Black Vote Photo – Say their Names – Henry Hezekiah Dee and Henry Smith.

The Black Vote Photo – Say their Names – Philando Castile and Quanice Hayes.

The Black Vote Photo – "Dream, Lead, Fight, Think, Write, Build, Speak, Educate, Believe, Challenge" like Martin, Harriet, Malcolm, Garvey, Maya, Madame CJ, Frederick, WEB, Thurgood and Rosa" to be "Bamma Free" like Me!"

WHO SPEAKS FOR THE BLACK VOTE IN THE AGE OF TRUMP?

The record shows, African-Americans have fought in every war America was a part of, from Crispus Attucks to World Wars One and Two with Dorian Miller "our Hero," then "Pork Chop Hill" in Korea, Vietnam and even Afghanistan and Iraq. Now the theater is Africa to extinguish the "bogey man" threatening America; nonetheless, the most potent and viable weapon we have is overwhelmingly the vote. While Malcolm X pointed to the "Ballot or Bullet" option, we recognize across today's political landscape the former is more potently effective if we use it wisely and consistently. Without question, we must hold both Democrats and Republican accountable. However, in this we must force Republicans to respect and contend with the Black vote while keeping Democrats' feet to the fire. Clearly, as Republicans continue to ignore Mr. Trump's 22,000 lies, falsity and pernicious shortcomings, the supposed illegitimacy of his election caused by Russian meddling in this sacred American institution practice, the consistent divisive and racist rhetoric, and as they process and band together to protect him in seeking to discredit the Muller and other investigations and inquiries, Black issues were not even considered. Thus, we must take a stand against the oppressor.

Therefore, we must play a more active role in unfolding circumstances and not be passive bystanders. As such then, if the Black vote turns out enmasse to **Spearhead** an effective coalition with the #Metoo Movement, Black Lives Matter, disrespected Latino voters, women across the spectrum, youth affected by gun violence and good and decent people, disrespected people of Mexican heritage, Muslims threatened by Trump's record, this combined effort can, as it did the 2018 Mid-term Election, hold Donald Trump in check, then send him and his Republican enablers packing in 2020.

"I appeal to all of you to get into this great revolution that is sweeping this nation. Get in and stay in the streets of every city, every village and hamlet of this nation until true freedom comes, until the revolution of 1776 is complete." **John Lewis**

"I say to people today, 'You must be prepared if you believe in something. If you believe in something, you have to go for it. As individuals, we may not live to see the end.'" **John Lewis**

8. LIFE IN DEATH: MEDGAR EVERS BY DR. FRED MONDERSON

Medgar Evers was murdered in his driveway because he chose to become active in voter registration.

Riding along Bedford Avenue in Brooklyn, New York, and viewing the mural gracing Medgar Evers College that read "Courage," "Strength," "Fortitude" an interesting thought crossed my mind. This individual, Medgar Evers is very much alive even though he is now a revered ancestor. Murdered for standing on principle, as a pillar of the Civil Rights struggle who fearlessly challenged the racial hatred and terrorism of his era and waged a voter register campaign, Medgar Evers refused to go quietly in the night. Because of his courage, tenacity, inspiration and the symbolism he represented, the founders who envisioned the significance of Malcolm-King resurrected this fearless leader and armed him, not with the deadly projectile that similarly ended his life and a selfless career of working for the betterment of others, but with an even more significantly potent device. That is, the mechanism of freedom of the mind, an educational institution that teaches the fundamentals designed to encourage creativity, create model-citizens, activists of all hues, and so engage in a perpetual state of grace through symbolism of freeing the shackled-mind of his people to become an influence and symbolism for the wider world. Alas, what more fitting form of employment for this "Light" than to be an educational "Torch Bearer" of intellectual inspiration and fortitude, especially in times of challenge, and, as Dr. King pointed to, controversy. After all, Victor Hugo held, "Beneath the tred of mighty armies, the pen is mightier than the sword" and "There is nothing mightier than an idea whose time has come."

People sometimes do stupid things that initially seem right though wrong, wherein the "Arc of the Moral Universe," in working its profound magic transforms such behaviors into a wonderfully creative expression forcing purveyors of evil wishing to recall their crass deeds but to no avail. It is as if in the sorrow of the experience Mr. Evers' family and community were sold lemon in which they creatively produced an elixir of intellectual lemonade that has quenched the thirst of ignorance and so for forty years; more than a generation, the symbolism and significance of Medgar Evers is still encouraging, directing and infusing untold numbers of young people with a tenacity to elevate themselves and make a constructive mark on society through purposeful and effective direction of the mind. There is thus, no greater gift the ancestors hoped for and welcome.

Malcolm X spoke of finding himself in prison but this is late; however, better late than never. What is significant; first, "Black Stalin" the Calypsonian monarch sang, "The more Africans they gun down, the more Africans keep coming." In that horrifying experience of their ever-continuing struggles that fell Dr. King, Malcolm X and Medgar Evers, not to forget the more than 100 unsolved civil rights murders, Blacks and the Black Vote must remain steadfast in determination to make the vote effective. It's clear, as all this unfolded, African people in America were forced to craft constructive and effective strategies to combat the depraved and intolerable conditions they were subjected to through Slave Trade and Slavery; the terrorist misfortunes throughout the Nadir, 1880-1930, in which Jim Crow, Ku Klux Klan activities, Sharecrop peonage, lack of jobs, all in face of national government abandonment of its citizens to which we must never forget that, "More than 100 unsolved civil right murders" and "4040 lynchings occurred in southern states from 1870 to 1950."

These were essentially and factually perpetrated by white men professing Christian principles and values, even as they took their wives and children and brothers and sisters to be witnesses to the murder of Black men, women and even children. Many of these victims' private parts were severed and doled out as souvenirs. Significantly, however, as the "Oppressor" today says, "Get back," we say, "No, fight back." In such a courageous stance, reinforced in ancestral wisdom through moral fortitude and philosophical support, the true nature of this psychological and spiritual soul-force actively crafted a methodology to combat the symbolism of fear and intimidation in the wanton killing of Black leaders. Realizing "sometimes no one cares" and the need to do for self, African-Americans endured the sorrow and responded in an unexpectedly and unbelievable manner to create something positive out of each such evil and tragedy.

The killing of the "Mother Emanuel 9" in South Carolina is a powerful example of hurt, grief, sadness, but the power of such forgiveness is a true example their tragic circumstances combatted and rejected the "ball and chain" burden of hate, as the victims' families quickly jettisoned that burdensome guilt in hating the killer, Dylan Roof. The world realized, he in turn has to live with not simply the folly of his actions; the mere crassness of his deed; but the fear, being in prison which has its principled rules, one day he may meet an untimely death, perhaps long before his state sponsored execution becomes due. The thought is so remindful of Jeffrey

Dahmer, the young man who killed and ate several Black victims and he was stoned to death on a labor rock pile in prison. This is perhaps the most inhuman way to die as the body is repeatedly wracked in the violent force of stone striking flesh, again and again. The thing about memorials is they pay tribute to sometimes fallen heroes cut short in the execution of their destiny or simply good people as those who did good things to benefit humanity and expired as their time on earth had ended. Remembering the good they had done, later their names were resurrected to grace structures, streets, even sailing vessels or the symbolism they stood for as it continues to inspire others in all walks of life. Fortunately, the tragedies and life experiences of Africans in America is replete with those glorious souls, revered ancestors, whose lives are still meaningfully benefitting not simply a single race but humanity in general. The question then becomes, where and when do we begin, in fact, continue to recognize and praise these individuals, even movements for the many ways, they benefited the human spirit. Even in protest mode, such memes as "No Justice, No Peace," "Whose Streets, Our Streets" have become global rally cries of people fighting for dignity and justice worldwide.

The Black Vote Photo – "The Brothers" "**BLACK LIVES MATTER**" – "We Will Breathe!"

The Black Vote Photo – "**BLACK LIVES MATTER**" – "Silence equals Violence."

The Black Vote Photo – Say their Names – India Kager and Irwin Pratt.

The Black Vote Photo – Say their Names – Quintonio Legrier and Rayshard Brooks.

The Black Vote Photo – "Black Lives Matter" and "Bamma Free" – Yes, "Black Lives Matter!"

Strange, an idea, a single phrase, never gets the recognition it deserves certainly by the people it is actually aimed at, even though it has taken flight, even across oceans, to become tools of liberation for people across the globe seeking justice and to redress grievances. Rather than beginning with the work of individuals, a focus on key terms sets the stage for better understanding of how ideas can galvanize people, become movements, challenge oppression and become effective change agents.

In looking at the challenging, yet glorious history of African-Americans, take for example Gabriel Prosser's statement after his revolt was betrayed proved even more profound in that he spoke truth to power saying, "What is all this farce of a trial. I know you intend to shed my blood. I have only one life to give for the salvation and liberation of my people. It is no different than what George Washington would have said if he was captured by the British. So, take me to the gallows and quickly end my life in cause of liberation of my people." The times and circumstances may be different, but in Officer Wilson killing of Michael Brown and his rationalization it was "Hulk Hogan against a five-year old," an idea soon forgotten because of its silly and perverted nature. Here we have a police officer, trained, equipped, been on the force for some time; yet, he refers to himself and perhaps thinks "as a five-year-old." Are we to believe his version of events, even that he is "a five-year-old?" Nevertheless, and in response, the galvanized young people's more creative expressions, "Hands up, Don't Shoot;" "Black Lives Matter;" "I am Michael Brown" were words of sentiments of power; if you will, "Ptahhotep 'Wisdom at the millstone.'" These shibboleths went viral globally, mobilizing demonstrations of young people in sympathy with this tragedy and wanting a world where people aspire to more equality in their expressions, treatment more just to echo Rodney King's pliant, "Can we all get along?"

The interesting thing about ideas as expressions, while some galvanized and sustain themselves, others issue an echo and streak across the heavens into oblivion. In 1941, A Philip Randolph, long in the field of Civil Rights activism and deploring the plight of African-Americans who had essentially voted democratic for the "New Deal" with little to show, spurred him into action. In apprising, rather reminding, the President of ongoing lynching, discrimination and lack of job opportunities for Blacks in AFL and in the War Industries, Mr. Randolph threatened to "March on Washington" if something was not done to address the problem of jobs and quality and equality of treatment. President Roosevelt listened attentively at the dinner, passed out cigars and told Mr. Randolph, "Go out there (in the streets) and make me do it." That is, peaceful protest to redress grievances is the American way.

But first, Marcus Garvey's "Look for me in the whirlwind," and "You have caged the lion, but the cubs are running free out there" expressed the deep conviction and the work and purpose of this great ancestor's ideas and influence. Even more important, the Red, Black and Green fluttering in wind and sunlight wherever especially at the African-American parade in Harlem, is a reminder the old lion is not really caged. Much more significant, however, in Minister Louis Farrakhan calling for the "Million Man March" on October 16, 1995, to see that same iconic Red, Black and Green flying proudly on the Capital Building alongside the Red, White and Blue, was truly a day of significance in more ways than one. Still and just as significant, that "Go out here" and "March on Washington" is a stark reminder there will be opposition to "Business as usual."

WHO SPEAKS FOR THE BLACK VOTE IN THE AGE OF TRUMP?

The Black Vote Photo – Marcus Garvey, the legendary "Nationalist and Pan-Africanist," hero through the ages here and abroad.

The Black Vote Photo – "Omega U" and more "Omega."

Though Malcolm X has passed on to ancestor glory, many are still inspired and enlightened with the enormous illumination his life and work represented. Let's not forget his "Ballot or Bullet" speech.

Equally, let's not forget, Dr. King and the "Big Six," with John Lewis numbered amongst them, marched in 1963 and announced the possibilities of a "Dream." In 2013, Reverend Al Sharpton, Dr. King's son, Martin III., Jesse Jackson, Marc Morial and thousands including Erik and Dad, returned to Washington to commemorate this historic event. And today, every 4th of April weekend, in commemoration of the death of Dr. King, when Al Sharpton and the **National Action Network** hosts their "Keeping the Dream Alive" promise activist forum, Congress, this is a reminder the "dream" is not yet achieved but countless numbers are in the field fighting to attain such. Importantly, however, Sharpton's efforts is not simply about meeting for discussion and forcing formulated policies but equally activist marches against Giuliani's brutal polices, expressing outrage against the tragedy of Sean Bell, the murderous death of Eric Garner, against the authorities handling events surrounding Michael Brown's killing, that of Travon Martin, Dorismond, Eleanor Bumpers and Amadou Diallo were all attempts to arouse the nation's and the world's conscience seeking to invoke legislative action to address wrong-doing and inequity but also to put the oppressor on notice, there's a price to pay, particularly through the economic boycott mechanism, not to forget the ballot box. While Malcolm put it forcefully, "The Ballot or the Bullet," Minister Louis Farrakhan more rightly made it clear, "Justice or Else!"

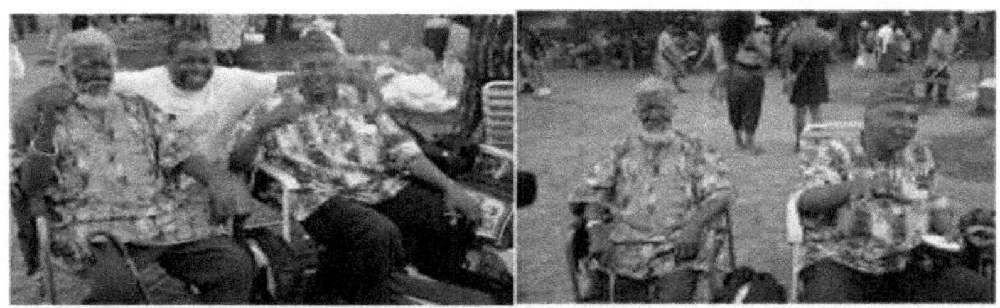

The Black Vote Photo – Dr. Jack Felder and Dr. Leonard Jeffries are joined by a bookseller from Harlem – And again, "**Stay Black**" but with more "**POWER**."

Powerfully, when Herman Ferguson insisted on Malcolm X's birthday, vendors on 125th Street in Harlem close for a set number of hours to honor the slain icon, there was some resistance but the potency of the idea was full of message that took root. Equally too, when the nationalist Sonny Carson chose to re-inter his great-uncle "The Runaway," Samuel Carson to Ghana, West Africa, opening the "Door of Return" and creating a site of pilgrimage for African-Americans seeking their "roots" anywhere in Africa, not only was this memorial a long time in coming as point of departure waiting for this symbol; this man, this time, we recognized that, the idea, the symbolism, the movement of "Life in Death" had "gone international."

Just as the **Negro Activist Anthem** "We shall overcome," even as uttered in the US Congress by President Linden Johnson following the death of John Kennedy and on eve of passage of the 1964 **Civil Rights Act** and the 1965 **Voting Rights Act**, it has been replaced today by "No Justice, No Peace" and "Whose Streets, Our Streets." These chants have similarly galvanizing potency becoming an international shibboleth for people seeking justice and equity in redress of grievances. This coming of age of activist mantras has been recognized, from the suffering, trials and tribulations of the struggles of African-Americans. Rightly then, this strategy has and continues to better the lot of humanity.

However, in all these efforts and circumstances let us not forget, Frederick Douglass' profound question, "What does the Fourth of July mean to a slave?" and that "Power concedes nothing without a struggle, it never did and it never will," are slogans that span decades and centuries. Such profound thoughts were contemporary with another historic ancestor, Harriet Tubman, the **Underground Railroad Conductor**, who insisted, she "never ran her train off the tracks," but boldly reminded her charges, "I would rather see you dead, than a slave." Even she recognized, however, "I could have saved more, if they only realized they were slaves." More significant, she insisted, "I must live free or die!"

Of equal significance, Marcus Garvey's "Africa for the Africans, those at home and those abroad," still resonates globally. His admonition was matched by W.E.B. DuBois' efforts as the "Father of Pan-Africanism," who recognized the 20th Century as the "Century of Race" or "color line." In that era of heightened Africanist activism, Booker T. Washington laid it down, "Pan-Africanism is the destiny of African people." And following, Kwame Nkrumah issued his insightful insistence, "Seek ye first the political kingdom and everything else will be added."

On the other side of the world in Guyana, President David Granger's recently declared, "No one can tell us who our heroes must be nor where we celebrate and locate our historic moments and monuments." Meanwhile, back home, Maulana Karenga the founder of **KWANZAA** enquired, asked, "Can you put something positive on Facebook?" In a challenge, however, Anthony Browder, more practically insisted, "Get off Facebook and put your face in a book!"

All this notwithstanding; the most potent idea to have been issued from the creative arsenal of the African-American experience has been the "Million Man Movement" and for this we have to thank Minister Louis Farrakhan and the **Nation of Islam**. The potency of this idea is not simply the message in the initial shibboleth but the frequency and multi-faceted nature of the tree morphing into a forest of activism, positive organizing and organizational building as the strategy continues to unfold in recurring "Million anniversaries." Imagine, millions of Black men, Black woman, and people of like minds convening on the grounds of the nation's capital, in recurring and proximate anniversaries to be recognized, speak truth to power and demand justice. Then, rejuvenated in the coordinated spirit of activism to return home and organize, educate our people and build on the momentum the Washington message delivered, perhaps President Johnson echoing the chorus "We shall overcome" reminds all concerned, Dr. King had been to the "Mountaintop" and rightfully exclaimed, "I may not get there with you, but I want you to know, we as a people will get to the promised land," for "Mine eyes have seen the glory of the coming of the Lord." His Truth Marches On!

The Black Vote Photo – "Solidarity" and "The King's Men" stand Tall!

The Black Vote Photo – Say their Names – Jamar Clark and Isiah Lewis.

The Black Vote Photo – Say their Names – Redel Jones and Regis Korchinski-Paquet.

The Black Vote Photo – “White Silence is Violence” and “Black Lives Matter,” “Equality,” “Black Love,” “Color is not a Crime,” “I Can’t Breathe,” “How many More?” “No Justice, No Peace,” “We Fighting …” “We Will Not Be Silenced” “Black Peace” – “Justice for Breonna Taylor” and “Black Lives Matter.”

“Vice-President Joe Biden and I believe we are in a fight to save the soul of this nation.” **John Lewis**

“We were beaten, we were tear-gassed. I thought I was going to die on this bridge. But somehow and some way, God almighty helped me here. We cannot give up now. We cannot give in. We must keep the faith, keep our eyes on the prize.” **John Lewis**

9. "SOUTHERN SHERIFFS" BY DR. FRED MONDERSON

Whether it was Rod Steiger or Archie Bunker who played Sheriff Gillespie as the lawman in the movie *In the Heat of the Night*, the Black detective had to enlighten him about the intricacies and perspectives of coming to correct conclusions regarding police work. This time, two contemporary sheriffs from South Carolina and Georgia are in the news not simply for exceptional performance of their jobs but equally for statements that many consider controversial with other implications. There is another sheriff from Arizona, who also came under scrutiny because of statements and the degree with which he executed his responsibilities as they relate to immigration and whether persons are legal residents or not. However, this latter official is not the focus of this essay; his case has been known, scrutinized and settled, sort of.

The South Carolina Sheriff recently questioned President Obama ordering the American flag lowered in honor of the passing of Nelson Mandela, one of the great leaders of the 20th Century. It is interesting, at the Memorial Service in South Africa in which President Obama and First Lady Michelle Obama represented this nation, he was accompanied by an American star-power delegation including former Presidents Jimmy Carter, William "Bill" Clinton, and George W. Bush. First Ladies Rosalind, Hillary and Laura, respectively accompanied their husband. Chelsea Clinton was also in attendance.

Nearly 100 world leaders, active and retired, came to pay their respect to a man whose life was like no other; a unique figure in history; who inspired the world through political and personal forgiveness and thus effectuated the power of unification in a land torn apart by the crimes of apartheid standing on the precipice of a destructive race war. In anticipation of this gathering and the solemn nature of the occasion, the President's actions were prudent policy.

The other Sheriff from Valdosta, Georgia pronounced the death of a very athletically active teen-ager, Kendrick Johnson ("KJ") as a tragic accident claiming the young man climbed into an enormous rolled-up floor mat in the gymnasium of his school. There, searching for his shoe, he ostensibly suffocated. An autopsy was performed and the family notified about the cause of death. Not satisfied with "the official version," for nearly a year, six days per week, the family staged a demonstration outside a local courthouse, bringing attention to the case and demanding more satisfactory answers. Finally, attention focused on their plight and a new interest ensued in efforts to get to the bottom of things.

Listening to the Steve Harvey Morning Show in New York on December 10, 2013, an attorney for the family; a Mr. Benjamin Crump who was the Trayvon Martin family attorney in that tragedy; informed on some troubling developments in the case. Mr. Crump explained the gymnasium area was under video coverage and in several angles the view was crystal clear where Mr. Johnson was clearly identified taking part in gym activities. However, the video covering that part of the gym where the potential "foul play" may have happened, where Mr. Johnson supposedly climbed into the rolled-up mat to retrieve his sneakers, that part of the film is very cloudy, essentially unidentifiable, useless. More important, however, when the family insisted on a more detailed report on the examination of the body, it turned out there was traces of blood, whose ownership the attorney did not specify. Additionally, examination of the exhumed body revealed the internal organs of Mr. Johnson were missing and his insides was stuffed with newspapers. Even more important, Mr.

Johnson's nails at the fingertips were all cut deep as if to remove all traces, potentially, of blood ostensibly indicating perhaps there was a struggle, he scratched someone and blood remained. Cutting off the fingertips was designed to get rid of potential DNA evidence.

Now, we know in the case of suspicious death, and not from natural causes, law-enforcement conducts extensive investigations to determine the cause or death. In the case of this very healthy teenager who played baseball, football and basketball, it stands to reason he did not die of natural causes! Given that law enforcement investigates and the now coming to light revelations regarding Mr. Johnson's end, it challenges the Sheriff's firm declaration as to the cause of death. It raises a question why he never became suspicious given the now revealed facts of the case; thus, one would wonder whether he is willing to stake his career on his official cause of death declaration? Was there a cover-up? Was the Sheriff ever suspicious of events? In this day and age, how could he believe the family would accept that coca-mammy story? How did he determine the kid crawled up into the folded-up mat? Again, given that law enforcement investigates, did the Sheriff put two and two together to arrive at 300? Does this sloppiness call into question other "causes of death" official reports of his office? All this forces us to wonder about the behaviors of "Southern Sheriffs" and others whose behaviors can certainly use some scrutiny, in fact, deserves more scrutiny.

WHO SPEAKS FOR THE BLACK VOTE IN THE AGE OF TRUMP?

Well, in terms of the South Carolina Sheriff who questioned the President of the United States' decision to fly the Stars and Stripes at half-mast, did he know the US has done so since 1957 for world leaders? Does this "whiting" trying to swim in "whale waters" realize such pronouncements are above his "pay grade?" Given such, is his pronouncement that the flag should only be flown at half-mast for Americans is actually an anti-Obama statement. Also, given South Carolina's history as home of the virulent anti-Obamaite Senator DeMint; uncensored "You lie" Congressman Joe Wilson; "Wishy Washy" or "Zig Zag" Senator Graham' and as Jessie Jackson exclaimed a few years ago, "South Carolina has 36 state prisons and 1 state college," with many Blacks confined in the former, as prison of the body, mind and soul how are statements of these kids received?. In a stretch of the imagination, the Sheriff could easily fit in "egregious cabals."

These associations, notwithstanding, the Sheriff is so wrong! The United States lowered the flag for Winston Churchill, Pope Paul II and several other deserving world leaders. The interesting this is, President Obama is a very intelligent visionary whose every action, decision has been questioned, challenged, some say even sabotaged by persons acting in a "treasonous" manner and all because the President is a Black man; and importantly, despite the virulent opposition designed to make his administration a failure. After all, Republican Senator Mitch McConnell expressly stated his goal "to make Barack Obama a one term President."

However, unable to prevent the President's re-election in 2012, Mr. McConnell never renounced his goal and *The New York Times* of October 6, 2013 expressly maintained and named individuals who met and planned to sabotage the President's every legislative and otherwise action on behalf of the American people! While this occurred after the 2012 election, every reason suggests the plot was put in place right after the 2008 election and all the principal players remained involved and named in the latest revelation.

Fast forward to the sorrowful passing of the South African leader and statesman and recognizing the personal strength of Mr. Mandela; as his health began to decline, President Obama instituted plans for a high-level American delegation to attend the funeral. This show of American Presidential star power consistent with lowering the flag was not simply above the South Carolina Sheriff's intellectual comprehension and pay grade, but as a stroke of genius he put America on the right side of history recognizing and tributing to what he called Mr. Mandela, "The last great liberator of the 20th Century."

The Black Vote Photo – "The Black Woman is the Black Man's Responsibility" and equally, "The Black Man is the Black Woman's Responsibility!"

The Black Vote Photo – "Get Your Knee Off Our Necks," says Lillian Baldwin and Kimberley Hanserd of Detroit, again!

The Black Vote Photo – Say their Names –Jamel Floyd and Jamee Johnson.

The Black Vote Photo – Say their Names – Rev. George Lee and Riah Milton.

The Black Vote Photo – "Black Lives Matter," "My Brother Matters" and "I am Black and My Life Matter" – "Justice for Jacob Blake, Breonna Taylor, George Floyd, Sandra Bland, Elijah McClain" while **BLM**.

Here was a man who "earned his place in history through struggle and took a stand on principle," to empower his nation through the vote. After the enormous suffering of South Africans for much of the 20th Century, Mr. Mandela's trials and tribulations; his lengthy prison incarceration, until global activism in its many ramifications forced the racist South African government to free this long serving prisoner, such actions are notable and deserve commendations. Upon his release, Mandela held no recriminations against the whites, urged his people to peacefully accept the transfer of power and exercise the long-sought after franchise.

To set the record straight, he established a **Truth and Reconciliation Commission** under Bishop Desmond Tutu and the Afrikaner Reverend Byers Naude, long a critic of Apartheid.

When all is said and done, Mr. Obama has always provided excellent leadership. Despite the enormous efforts expended to sabotage his presidency, Mr. Obama always lead in the best interest of the American people and nation. History has always been the best judge of leaders and their tenure and as it has judged Mr. Mandela, so too it will judge Mr. Obama as well as the Southern Sheriffs, those mentioned here and others whose performance will ultimately become public record.

"To make it hard, to make it difficult almost impossible for people to cast a vote is not in keeping with the democratic process." **John Lewis**

"John Lewis was the patron saint of the right to vote."
David Brinkley

10. ORIGINAL BOYS WEARING HOODS BY DR. FRED MONDERSON

Make no mistake the "Original Boys Wearing Hoods" were members of the Ku Klux Klan and many have argued they metamorphosed into elements of the "Tea Party" Movement's conservatism as a new assertion of the Klan, born of a hatred that never seems to end! Suppressed by the federal government's use of marshals and troops authorized under the **Force Acts of 1870 and 1871**, the Klan's terrorism was halted during **Reconstruction** though it was replaced by "Jim Crowism" and similar sinister strategies in alliance with the southern white power structure who influenced poor whites through the notion of white supremacy against political action by the newly freed African-American. However, by 1915, the year the "Grandfather Clause" was repealed, the Klan rose again to fight, as Unger states, "for native born, white, gentile Americans" against Negroes, Jews, Catholics and foreigners. By the end of World War, I Klan members were incensed by Black soldiers returning from Europe, as Lerone Bennett, Jr. says in *Confrontation*: *Black and White* (1966: 121) because Blacks had been "killing white men and sleeping with white women." In the post-war years, they gained attention by distributing literature and selling Klan paraphernalia; so much so, membership increased to more than five million members in the 1920s. But, as Unger (1971: 120) writes further, "By 1927, however, the Klan had begun to overreach itself and its excesses of violence and vigilante tactics, as well as the corrupt and immoral behavior of some of its leaders, repelled many Americans. By the end of the decade, it had declined leaving behind an ugly legacy of hatred and violence endorsed in the name of one hundred percent Americanism."

Nevertheless, this terror group continued to function somewhat openly, somewhat under cover, though somewhat checked by strategies of Black assertiveness and many believe the election of Barack Obama galvanized that brotherhood of sinister behavior; only at this later time the hoods were replaced by casuals and business suits, still in the name of conservatism. However, while the Civil War Amendments were designed to free and empower the ex-slave, southern conservatism engaged a number of devious strategies to regain power and limit Black new-found political effectiveness. In one instance, Irwin Unger's *American History II: Reconstruction to Present*, New York: Monarch Press (1971: 7) ties southern Conservatives to the Ku Klux Klan in the following statement: "Some of these Southern Conservatives were happy to use the regular political process to achieve their ends. Others were willing to use violence and intimidation against Scalawags, Carpetbaggers, and Negroes. The more violent conservatives organized groups like the Ku Klux Klan, a secret society founded in 1866 to help 'redeem' the South from Radicals, black and white. The Klan was most active between 1868 and 1870 when its members, dressed in white sheets and hoods, threatened, beat and even killed supporters of the Radical state governments."

This was generally in response to events of 1867 in which, as Lerone Bennett in *Before the Mayflower* (1964) (1978: 196) wrote: "During the summer and fall of 1867, the Negro masses were stirred by an unparalleled ferment of political activity. Negroes flocked to huge open-air meetings, registered and organized political groups. Leaders emerged from the masses and demanded political and civil equality.

The white South was stunned. It was believed at first that 'Sambo' would fall flat on his face. But the freedmen disappointed their late masters: They demonstrated a real genius for what one writer called 'the lower political arts.'" Explaining Klan origins and intent, Bennett (1978: 196-197) continued further, that the first national meeting of the Klan occurred in April 1867, Room 10 at the Maxwell House in Nashville where in attendance were: "Confederate generals, colonels, substantial men of church and state, from Georgia, from Alabama, from all over. The leader: Nathan Bedford Forest, the strong man of the Fort Pillow Massacre. The plan: reduce Negroes to political impotence. How? By the boldest and most ruthless political operation in American history. By stealth and murder, by economic intimidation and political assassination, by whippings and maimings, cuttings and shootings, by the knife, by the rope, by the whip. By the political use of terror, by the braining of the baby in its mother's arms, the slaying of the husband at his wife's feet, the raping of the wife before the husband's eyes. By fear! Soon the South was honeycombed with secret organizations: The Knights of the White Camelia, the Red Shirts, the White League, Mother's Little Helpers and the Baseball Club of the First Baptist Church."

In a somewhat prejudiced analysis attempting to explain the above dynamics, William Dunning of the "Dunning School" at Columbia University, according to Norman Hodges's *Black History*, New York: Monarch Press (1974: 113) theorized an interpretation on influential events in the South following the Civil War, of which the last of five states now, "driven to desperation by misrule, the long suffering Southerners formed vigilante groups like the Ku Klux Klan to rescue the region from the carpetbagger regime." Hodges (1974: 113) continued his insight by stating further: "Morison has summed up the imagery of the Dunning interpretation in these words: 'The accepted fable represents Reconstruction as the ruthless attempt of Northern politicians to subject the white South, starving and helpless, to an abominable rule by ex-slaves … and from which it was rescued by white-hooded knights on horseback who put the Negro 'back where he belonged.'" However, in *The Afro-American in United States History* (1972: 211-212) Da Silva, Finkelstein and Loshin remind us in this new advantage, "the men who gained power in Southern local and state governments could do much as they pleased. The power of the Federal government was not used to protect rights. That left each town, county or state its own master. The KKK and groups like it could attack a black person without fear of real punishment. The men who owned newspapers in the south began to work with the political leaders and KKK groups. They filled the minds with Jim Crow ideas. Terror silenced all men, white and black, who could not agree with them. They forced all of the south to accept Jim Crow." In this, "White men in the south built a wall between themselves and all blacks. They did this by laws and customs that pushed black people lower and lower. Rich and poor whites worked together to make this wall higher and higher.

Rich men did it so they could keep their wealth and power. Poor whites did it to feel better than someone – in his case the Afro-American." Today we ask, 'Is that where we're heading' as we listen to the rhetoric of the conservative right wing, led by the Circus Ring Master Donald Trump, himself?

The Black Vote Photo – "At Dr. King's Memorial" and "**NAN** reminds of **Lives Lost**!"

WHO SPEAKS FOR THE BLACK VOTE IN THE AGE OF TRUMP?

The Black Vote Photo – Say their Names – James Chaney and James Jahar Perez.

The Black Vote Photo – Say their Names – Ricky Javonta Ball and Ronnie Lee Shorter.

The Black Vote Photo – At Dr. King's Memorial, "My Brother Matters" and "Black Lives Matters" and "Black Books," "Black Films," "Black Music," "Black Art," "Black TV," "Black Plays," "Black People," **BLACK EVERYTHING**!"

Thus, as "forward to the Past" Newt Gingrich and "Poison the well" Rick Santorum vied to be considered the most conservative, one has to wonder if this is where they wanted to take the Negro and the nation? However, that is probably where we are under Donald Trump and his lies, racist vision, effete leadership, etc. After all, and we must never forget, as Hodges (1974: 117) writes: "The historical record strongly supports the view that the former rebel White South was unrepentant and vengeful in its treatment of Blacks during the two years of home rule that followed in the wake of war (1865-1867). A Black doctor, Daniel Norton, of Williamsburg, Virginia, described the situation to a Congressional Subcommittee, in 1866 [where he stated]: '… the spirit of the whites against the blacks is much worse than it was before the war …" In addition, he declared Klan behavior was such that blacks 'would be in danger of being hunted and killed.' In many respects, a century and a half later this attitude has continued though the law has more vigorously prosecuted such practitioners. Today the murder of George Floyd and similar situations, and protesting reaction may lead many to believe, we have in fact arrived at the hell-station. After all, Donald Trump did tell Bob Woodward, he felt no compassion on ill-treatment of Blacks and "did not drink the cool aid."

If we explore this some more, we recognize it's a fact, "Newspapers tell the story of a nation" and that "One picture can tell a thousand words" but equally one movie can graphically implant images in the mind that, on the one hand, paints a picture of events but also send a message of past issues or a reminder to others of returning to behaviors of the past. Take for example, the movie **Ten Commandments**, perhaps the most shown of all produced films; about ancient Egypt but purportedly shot in Arizona and seen thousands of times around the world; it is a great distortion yet considered "gospel" in the minds of many. Additionally, Dr. Yosef ben-Jochannan always railed about social upheaval events in this nation that preceded the return showing of **Gone with the Wind**, while the book **The Klansman** by Thomas Dixon is another example of a moving tale, depicted in the movie **Birth of a Nation** portray Klan misdeeds. In *Race: The History of An Idea in America* (1963) (1968: 339-340) Thomas F. Gossett writes, **Birth of a Nation's** "version of history is frankly and crudely racist. The last half of the movie deals with the horrors of carpetbagger and Negro rule in South Carolina during the **Reconstruction**. Negroes are shown wildly reveling at elections, voting with both hands, and keeping the white man from the polls by force. As members of the state legislature, Negroes sit with their hats on and their bare feet on the desks as they drink liquor from flasks and pass an intermarriage law. The leading white Radical Reconstructionist in the North is shown with his Negro mistress. In the climax of the film, a renegade Negro pursues a young white girl through the woods. In order to avoid rape, she leaps to her death from a high rock. Her brother leads a mob to lynch the Negro and then organize a unit of the Ku Klux Klan to regain control of society by white men. He breaks up a crowd of rioting Negroes just in time to save another white girl from forced marriage with the mulatto lieutenant-governor. The film was one of the great box-office successes of all time; millions of Americans flocked to see it and to absorb its 'message'"

The Black Vote Photo – "Stolen Outta Africa" and "Black Woman, Tigress!"

WHO SPEAKS FOR THE BLACK VOTE IN THE AGE OF TRUMP?

The Black Vote Photo – "Dreamers" and "The Dream!" Strange, we never see Donald Trump in fitness training, but too busy working, to **GOLF**!

Even Gene Hackman's movie **Mississippi Burning** painted a grim reality of events that is a powerful reminder of behaviors still not extricated from the history or current practicing mindset of some in this nation.

Recently, within the last week, the movie **Oh Brother**, **Where Art Thou** was shown on a local channel. While the general theme said one thing, thousands of words of a photograph and one million of a movie enables people with vision to see the subliminal messages extrapolated from imaged realities past and present.

One particular scene in **Oh Brother**, while it never got to that horrifying scene of a "hung and burning black man" as in **The Great Debaters**, or as in **The Black Book** showing "a roasting black man" surrounded by jeering white men, the movie scene depicts the Ku Klux Klan in full panoply, battledress, white uniforms, in measured formation in white headgear as the "Original Boys Wearing Hoods." While a seeming glimpse of a colorful spectacle, the scene is actually a microcosm of longstanding practice of terrorism against the African enslaved then freed in America, dehumanized and debased in a system practicing lynchings, tar and feathers, intimidation, denial of human and civil rights, Blacks discriminated against at the ballot box and even killed before they received a sub-standard education. So much so, commentators have labeled the decades following the Civil War that destroyed the system perpetuating the "Crime against humanity" within the **Institution of Slavery** as the "Classic Age of American domestic terrorism." This is because institutions of men on horsebacks and in hoods, particularly in collaboration with the white southern elite spewed carnage against black men, women and children in this nation as they sought to instill and reinforce a false notion of white supremacy. What was not apparent at the time, contrary to some theorists, the African or Negro in America was never inferior mentally but got inferior treatment in a land that boasted of freedom and equality. Equally too and a fact that should never be overlooked, Blacks were trained and sent overseas to defend this nation and many came home as WEB Dubois reminded, "we went abroad fighting and we come home fighting."

Another interesting thing about **Oh Brother**, it reinforced the view of Ku Klux Klan as an organized and regimented racist movement and system. However, like all organisms in nature, these do not terminate themselves but evolve in strategy, tactics, make-up, all forcefully albeit, designed to perpetuate their founding philosophy. In this manner they attract new converts to their way of thinking despite new generations' attempts to distance themselves from that disdainful past.

The CBS public affairs program **60 Minutes** ran an episode of the FBI investigating one of more than one hundred unsolved Civil Rights murder cases in Mississippi and elsewhere in the South. The subject of one case in particular was still alive but no one was talking except the victim's family members. The FBI's lead detective did explain, in the climate of the time, anyone who wanted to run for any office had to be a member or espouse the philosophy of the hooded terrorist groups as the KKK, Knights of the White Camellia, White Citizens Council, and so on. None of these groups truly disbanded, revoked their philosophy or left their area of operation. They may have gone underground, changed their tactics and their attire "from hoods to business suits," then studied the law to more effectively get around it and been elected to government as conservatives serving as clogs in the system or patronage mills for people of similar minds, yet still continuing to recruit members and practice their racist agenda. Thus, thinking people must wonder, particularly when presidential candidates, seeking to unseat Presidents, as in the case of Barack Obama tell how conservative they are, one has to wonder, is there a connection with past terrorism?

While this at the time of the Clinton and Trump debates did not seem apparent; by now, some four years later, Donald Trump's lies, divisiveness, racist action and sayings, poor leadership seems to indicate prophecy and aspirations manifested. Despite his false pronouncements about helping Black Americans, his statements, Michael Cohen's assertion he is a racist, equally his sister and niece's revelation that he is a racist is ample proof that he is!

The Black Vote Photo – "Sure, **BLACK LIVES MATTER**" equally, **Justice or Else**!

WHO SPEAKS FOR THE BLACK VOTE IN THE AGE OF TRUMP?

The Black Vote Photo – "I get mad about **Kneeling on Necks**, not Football fields."

"The final responsibility of history is the responsibility of scholars of African descent." John Henrik Clarke. **Address to the Regional Conference on Afro American History**. University of Detroit. (May 11-13, 1967), "A New Approach to African history."

"I believe race is too heavy a burden to carry into the 21st century. It's time to lay it down. We all came here in different ships, but now we're all in the same boat." **John Lewis**

"He was young, with a charming personality who had so much love." Said of **John Lewis**

"Don't Boo! Vote!" **Barack Obama**

11. VOTING RIGHTS AND REDISTRICTING BY DR. FRED MONDERSON

Attorney General Eric Holder gave an interesting speech on Tuesday December 13, 2011 at the Lyndon B. Johnson library in which he took on the issue of redistricting that has been causing some concern across the South as the nation geared up for the 2012 national elections. President Johnson, who signed the 1965 Voting Rights Act, would have been proud of Mr. Holder whose Justice Department promised to move aggressively in reviewing, according to *The New York Times*, Wednesday December 14, 2011, in which Charlie Savage's "Holder signals Tough Review of State Laws on Voting Rights" – "Voting laws that civil rights advocates say will dampen minority participation in next year's election." Pulling no punches and promising to use the full weight of his Department to ensure that new electoral laws are not discriminatory, the Attorney General held protecting ballot access for all eligible voters "must be viewed not only as a legal issue but as a moral imperative." Thereupon he called on all Americans to urge their "political parties to resist the temptation to suppress certain votes in the hope of attaining electoral success and, instead achieve success by appealing to more voters."

For some time now, attention has been focusing on voting rights as it has been affected through redistricting which occurs every ten years after the census count. The argument has been made that the dominant political party in state legislatures tends to redraw the lines in a manner that benefits that party's incumbent members and the new candidates they intend to field. This method of manipulating the political boundaries has been called Gerrymandering after an original theorist called Jerry. Apparently, such an individual had been assigned to draw up a particular voting district and he skewed the configuration to such an extent, one observer remarked the new district lines looked very much like a salamander. The author then responded, "This is not a salamander, it is a gerrymander!" The name stuck and so any attempt to carve unusual district voting lines that include certain groups or exclude or hinder others, is considered "Gerrymandering." However, while this "pre-carving" may not be considered illegal, it certainly is unethical and immoral in that it seeks to diffuse, limit or diminish the voting strength of one or more groups to aid or advance the cause of another to give that group an edge at upcoming elections.

Gerrymandering is not the only way in which the voting strength and *ipso facto* voting power of different, albeit minority, groups are targeted as part of a general strategy of disfranchisement and voter suppression. In various regions of the country people convicted of a felony are deprived of their voting rights. Some have argued in several southern states the criminal justice system is used as a mechanism to disfranchise minorities who disproportionately comprise prison populations. In this, the argument has been made that misdemeanor criminal behavior is oftentimes elevated to felony standard and as such these individuals are removed from the voting rolls. Advocates for these dispossessed persons have argued, once a person has paid the debt to society then all of these natural and civil as well as political rights should be reinstated.

Another method used to purge the voting rolls is to insist people who have not voted in recent elections be deemed ineligible. However, while this may create a gray area, nefarious individuals with a party agenda often take the initiative and remove persons in this and other unscrupulous moves. This form of behavior is a throwback to the past Civil War era when southern voting and polling individuals went to great lengths to deny and invalidate the intent of the 13th,

14th and 15th Amendments that followed the conflict. To recall, southern polling officials required of freedmen that they take literacy tests, show proof of property qualification, evidence of paid poll taxes and they even invented a "grandfather clause" which held, if one's grandfather had voted, then regardless of one's literacy, intellectual or other qualifying factors, they were entitled to vote. Naturally, Blacks who had been enslaved and denied the ballot previously were automatically disqualified while whites who cod not muster the literacy test were given a pass. For more than four decades the "Grandfather clause" held sway and helped and hurt voters until it was declared unconstitutional by the Supreme Court in 1915. At the John Lewis funeral Memorial, the former President Barack Obama commented on "guessing how many jelly beans are in a jar," as a Southern, **Jim Crow Era**, right to vote. Matching these "legal machinations" of voting denial, threats and intimidation in face of a national government turning a deaf ear, black voting rights had been effectively nullified and a manipulated "White Primary" further alienated and restricted those who were hardy enough to attempt to exercise the franchise.

History has shown evidence of white men with guns at polling stations and this was designed to intimidate black voters. The secret nature of the ballot was betrayed and an individual's voting preference was reported to his employer the next day almost certainly to get him fired from a hard-won job. In addition, signs indicating polling sites were often turned around sending voters in the wrong direction to be often waylaid by highwaymen as all part of the conspiracy to nullify black and other minorities' votes. These sinister deeds do not exhaust efforts to block legitimate black ballot expression. What is interesting, as later as the 2008 national election, Republicans engaged in similar dishonest practices, insisting on "Day One" Republicans vote and on "Day Two" Democrats vote. This was designed to confuse persons not really astute about the process. People were informed if they had outstanding warrants or parking tickets the police would be there to arrest them if they tried to vote. People's jobs were threatened if they tried to vote and a whole lot more strategies were used to dissuade would-be voters who tended to vote democrat. In addition to the above, disqualification methods may be mentioned "mental incompetents, election law violator and vagrants."

While the 13th Amendment freed the slaves, the 14th gave citizenship to persons born in the United States and the 15th Amendment (1968), adopted in 1870, forbade any state from denying persons the right to vote because of race, color, or previous condition of servitude. Jack C. Plano and Milton Greenberg in *The American Political Dictionary* (1962) (1989: 71) summed up the significance of the Fifteenth Amendment. To explain this, they wrote: "Although the Fifteenth Amendment does not give anyone an absolute right to vote, it does prohibit any discrimination because of race or color. Not until recent years have blacks made significant advances in realizing the goals established by the amendment. In 1960, for example, the Supreme Court ruled that the racial gerrymandering of Tuskegee, Alabama, so as to exclude all Black voters from city elections violated the Fifteenth Amendment (*Gomillion v. Lightfoot*, 364 U.S. 339). The Civil Rights Acts of 1957, 1960, 1964 and the Voting Rights Act of 1965, 1970, and 1975 was passed by Congress and the Twenty-Fourth Amendment prohibiting poll taxes was adopted to aid backs in overcoming the various devices used by some southern states to frustrate the purposes of the Fifteenth Amendment." It may well be that history has repeated itself as gerrymandering is being driven in the rush to redistrict in the several states and as such Attorney General Eric Holder's intervention was not only timely, but necessary.

Today, purportedly behind his challenger Joe Biden, Mr. Trump has raised another issue of voter suppression, albeit fraud, because of the ensuring pandemic and the problems regular voting poses. Many states proposed voting by mail-in-ballot. Strange, the president and many of his principal backers voted absentee; viz., by mail; yet, he rails against this. A principal reason, even he gives, is since mail-in voting is generally, universal, essentially, if too many people vote, Republicans can't win.

We recognize time is up for the process of redrawing political boundaries based on the newest census data that is due to determine how recourses and representation in local school board, city council, county commission and state legislatures will be apportioned. However, what led to the Attorney general's intervention is the manner several state legislatures under Republican control seem to rush to target black areas that potentially vote democratic.

The Black Vote Photo – Folks just enjoying the view of protesters leaving the Martin Luther King, Jr. Memorial with the DC Memorial in the rear- and more with a sign that reads – "Selling Cigarettes Outside A Store – Eric Garner!"

The Black Vote Photo – Scan to Vote; Sign the Petition - BLM;" – "Justice for Jacob Blake!"

WHO SPEAKS FOR THE BLACK VOTE IN THE AGE OF TRUMP?

The Black Vote Photo – Say their Names – James Scurlock and Janet Wilson.

The Black Vote Photo – Say their Names – Ryan Stokes and Sahlah Ridgeway.

The Black Vote Photo – While we may insist by saying "Enough," The big Question is – "Am I next? that is a very good question"

The Black Vote Photo – "When Mr. Lincoln's "Slaves" rebelled they crowded his Memorial.

The Black Vote Photo – Now tie these two images to "Surgical spending of Black Dollars" and see how quickly reform will come through passage of meaningful legislation for John Lewis Voting Rights Renewal and George Floyd Police Brutality Act.

"I say to people today, 'You must be prepared if you believe in something. If you believe in something, you have to go for it. As individuals, we may not live to see the end.'" **John Lewis**
"The essence of the American story is John Lewis."

"In John Lewis we have lost a powerful voice for what is right, just and true." **Bakari Sellers**

12. LAWMAKERS IN HOODIES BY DR. FRED MONDERSON

Taking the law into their own hands, several lawmakers have made a clear and unmistakable statement by wearing a "Hoodie" on the floor of their legislature. First, the *New York Post* of Tuesday March 27, 2012 featured a photograph of New York State Senators Kevin Parker, Bill Perkins and Eric Adams wearing Hoodies "in Albany yesterday in tribute to Trayvon" which said "The demonstration of minorities by policies was born here in New York City!" Now, and however, Congressman Bobby Rush (D. Illinois) has been removed from the U.S. House of Representatives chamber for wearing a "Hoodie" on the floor of that legislative body while giving a speech on Trayvon Martin, the young man shot to death by Neighborhood-Watch Volunteer George Zimmerman. The significance of such social protest within a legislative body seems designed to call attention for government to more closely view this case, examine existing laws that actually undercut citizens' rights and equality by even more serious undercurrents taking Black-Americans more seriously.

Every American takes pride in their ethnic heritage and so does the African-American. When Barack Obama declared his candidacy for the Presidency of the United States, having declared his ethnicity, African-Americans took great pride in seeing a Black man with a Black wife and two lovely daughters representing the best of an American family. They turned out in droves to vote Mr. Obama for President to be part of the historic moment when the nation elected its first African-American to the nation's highest office. After all, we have experienced the first Black Governor, Senator, Congressman, Police Captain, Corrections Officer, General, Admiral,

Cabinet Member and so much more. Therefore, many argued, the nation was ready for a Black President, Commander-In-Chief with a Black First Lady and a Black First Family. Many people hailed this as the beginning of a "post-racial America." However, subsequent events proved this was wishful thinking because of the many "fifth wheels to the coach" and the numerous individuals setting backfires that did nothing but agonize the soul of this nation.

Many people argued the birth of the "Tea Party Movement" was an outgrowth of the Ku Klux Klan with the same racist outlook as they evolved from white hoods to business suits. As they caricatured the President, observers noticed the racial animosity in the attacks. Yet, Mr. Obama, smart as he is and more American than most of the critics of his birthright and patriotism, dismissed those roasting simply as imitations of "youthful temper tantrums." However, others saw a more sinister side to it. African-Americans complained, "Look at how they are treating the President, our hero!" The "Tea Party" attacked the President! They questioned his birthright, his religion, his patriotism, his leadership skills, his right to be Commander-In-Chief, his sincerity, his numbers and his judgment. No one said anything to challenge this venomous behavior from in and outside of government. Race baiters accused the President of going to change the Constitutional right to bear arms and in response they stocked up on armaments in preparation for a race war they thought would come, but didn't.

Much of Donald Trump's tirade is a carbon copy of these ugly and racist sentiments.

When Mr. Obama set about tackling the many challenges facing the American nation such as profuse job loss, home foreclosures, Wall Street in rapid retreat, the auto industry failing miserably, deterioration of social and physical infrastructure, education in decline, housing starts and mortgages "underwater," and while two wars waged in Iraq and Afghanistan, with Al Qaeda terrorists threatening, Somali Pirates abducting on the high seas and the world angry at the image of America, he got no cooperation from Republicans. Despite the trumping of every conceivable anti-Obama sentiment the President was proved successful in tackling nearly ninety percent of those listed maladies despite "I got that Nigger" thumbs up Senator Mitch McConnell's mandate to make Mr. Obama "a one term president;" Jim DeMint wanted to create his "Waterloo;" and every Republican lined-up in total opposition to the President and his policies.

The Black Vote Photo – On the Steps of the Lincoln Memorial – "Black Lives Matter" and more "Black Lives Matter" marchers.

The Black Vote Photo – “I will Vote,” “Biden-Harris 2020” and “Breonna Taylor.”

Thus, the fight to gain, sustain and exercise that quintessential American privilege, the right to vote has been fraught with challenges, setbacks, coinciding with expressions of job losses, more setbacks; yet, Blacks expressed a resolute determination that there’s no turning back now! As the US Marines say, “We don’t go back, we go forward!” This journey began with the 14th Amendment granting citizenship to persons born in America or naturalized establishing a basis for 15th Amendment entitlement granting the right to vote to American males. Females won the right to vote in 1920, some 52 years later, though most whites possessed the right to vote; yet Blacks had to wait.

Given their history, the right to vote for the first time instantly saw Black political power experience peaks and valleys resulting from the new freedom. So much so, when unimpeded, voter registration mounted substantially and Blacks were elected to local and state legislatures and so began leveling the political landscape, rewriting state Constitutions and sending representatives to the national government in Washington, DC. In protecting and utilizing the vote, they began making educational inroads benefitting the freedman and his offsprings, even supporting land ownership. However, much of this has been under threat from that early time to today.

The Black Vote Photo – "Biden for President 2020."

The Black Vote Photo – "Folks taking a rest along the Marching Trail" and "Hair Like Wool!"

"Before we went on any protest, whether it was sit-ins or the freedom rides or any march, we prepared ourselves, and we were disciplined. We were committed to the way of peace - the way of non-violence – the way of love – the way of life as the way of living." **John Lewis**

"The country lost a Hero and an Icon in John Lewis."

"John Lewis was a fighter for equality and justice."

13. HONORING JOHN LEWIS BY DR. FRED MONDERSON

To truly appreciate the life and legacy of John Lewis, we can begin with one of his most profound admonitions, "We must vote like we have never voted before." If Black-Americans voted at 82 percent for Barack Obama in 2008, then to Honor John Lewis we must top this yardstick by pulling the voting lever as it if to pull down rather than sustain the Trump statue.

From what we know today, July 18, 2020, a credible question to be asked is, 'How could any self-respecting Black person vote for Donald J. Trump in November 2020?" While this question equally applies to white voters, because this book is about the Black Vote, its restricted to this ethnic group, given Mr. Trump once boasted, "96 percent of Blacks will vote for me in 2020." The man is a pathological liar so this figure is wrong! One placard, carried in the post-George Floyd murder protest read, "If you're not mad, they you're not paying attention."

A driving motive behind **Black Solidarity Day**, the first Monday in November, beside the dynamics of "Don't go to work, don't shop, demonstrates a profound show of self-love and Black unity, then the next day, Tuesday, election day, turn out in record numbers and vote for your candidate of choice."

Back in January 2016, Representative James Clyburn, battling in the belly of the Congressional beast, admonished a Forum held by Rev. Al Sharpton in Washington, DC., with he, Clyburn, stated, "This is the most consequential election of our time." Many persons, unhappy with Donald Trump's opponent, Hillary Clinton, either did not vote in that year's national election or voted to take a chance on

Donald Trump, hence his election. Notwithstanding, the baggage he brought to Election Day, in 4 years, the world has seen the racism, evil, even lack of empathy that represents the true reality of President Trump' integrity or lack thereof, arrogance and poor leadership, but more important, his unrelenting insistence and unquenched desire to get and hold power, at all costs; and so tramples upon the Constitution, the nation's bedrock of law. His shameful division of the nation along racist lines is equally appalling as his response to the Carona Virus.

Continuously demonstrating arrogance, bombast and insensitivity, he now wants to be re-elected to lead this nation and the western alliance despite his demonstrated lack of leadership skills, yet full of divisive hate-driven disposition that is dividing the nation. Let's not forget, John Bolton remined, every action, thought, statement of Donald Trump as president was designed to enhance his chance of being re-elected, not necessarily to lead but possibly more important, to benefit the Trump Organization financially. Providing no leadership on Carona-Virus pandemic, he yet pushed to re-open the nation's economy and weeks later the Virus re-emerged with a vengeance across the southern states, where much of Mr. Trump's base resides. These are the areas he pushed the most to rapidly open and these areas are in crisis today, for as he told Bob Woodward as early as February 6, 2020, the Virus is five time more lethal than the flu; yet, he hid this from the American people, particularly his base, holding large rallies with no mast and social distancing, exposing the, to perils of the disease. Now he trumpets school re-opening, within weeks, while offering no coherent and viable national plan to safeguard the young in an age of pandemic. That lack of leadership he so relishes in on the issue of masks, his base following his unfocused realization of the dangers of the pandemic while ignoring the science and scientists who are experts in these issues; he further exposes his people, actually the nation, to a deadly pandemic spiraling out of control, claiming more lives, and alarming the world who so often looked to American ingenuity to address most major problems.

Mr. Trump's weak and ineffective leadership and his pathological lying dictates Americans should not believe anything he says or does given the intent is not the nation's but his own interest, particularly financial, that is! A recent poll indicated; 64 percent of Americans do not trust what the President says about the Carona virus. In fact, from June 6th to July 5th, Mr. Trump made some 41 false statements about the Carona-virus, for an average of some 7 false statements per day. Now, where is the leadership, where is the guidance, where is the truthfulness of a leader, where is the leadership his position craves. Why does Mr. Trump divide rather than unite the nation at this most critical time in its greatest tragedy? Fact is, Mr. Trump panders to the base that, in a region of racist and deadly action, has an unhealthy dose of the Pandemic illnesses and deaths.

WHO SPEAKS FOR THE BLACK VOTE IN THE AGE OF TRUMP?

It is one thing to be a forgiving people; but "Shame on you the first time; and Shame on me the next time;" is a meaningful yardstick to dictate future action. Mr. Trump's "Only I" mantra which resulted in some 22,000 lies, approaching nearly 200,000 deaths from Carona-Virus related maladies, divisive rhetoric that pits groups at each other, staunch defense of Confederate traitors' statues because they were Southern are among significant issues to consider before election. One commentator, focusing on the Pandemic response noted, Mr. Trump rapidly mobilized to protect Confederate statues but the medical community is hurting because of insufficient testing and shortages of PPP and other equipment he has not provided to fight the virus. These are all indications Mr. Trump is a "bad penny" and must be discarded.

If that is not enough, compare the present campaign ads of the two candidates. While Joe Biden demonstrates calm in a reasoned approach "To save the soul of the nation;" Donald Trump projects mayhem, destruction of property and chaos if the other guy wins. He offers no constructive plan that offsets Bidens. This is a further example of the "Only I" falsity by this "Johnny Come Lately Super Patriot," who when given the opportunity to serve his country in the military complained of his "bone spurs" and got educational deferment from serving. Trump refuses to realize much of the images he projects in his ads, were a result of developments that occurred on his watch, as a result of his in-action and poor leadership. As a "wartime President" he is in denial. Biden says of the "War time President" he has "surrendered" though he feels safe in the White House Bunker.

In regard the pandemic's rising infection cases, mounting hospitalizations and increased death toll, CNN's John King quoting *The Washington Post*, the reason the President is not focused on the virus, "he doesn't want to be distracted!" This is the same as his lying by not telling the American people about the airborne nature and deadly form of the Virus as he told Bob Woodward. Claiming he did not want to spread panic, he does this so well in frightening Suburbia, fanning flames about Portland and Kenosha as he did about the "Caravans" at time of the 2018 Midterm- election. Running on his "businessman" mantra; fact is, he filed for bankruptcy five times in his career, among other misgivings. This is the man who wants to be re-elected to lead the nation.

The Black Vote Photo – At "Dr. King's Memorial" (left) and Lillian Baldwin and Kimberley Hanserd (right) insist "Get Your Knee Off Our Necks" with the Washington Monument in the rear.

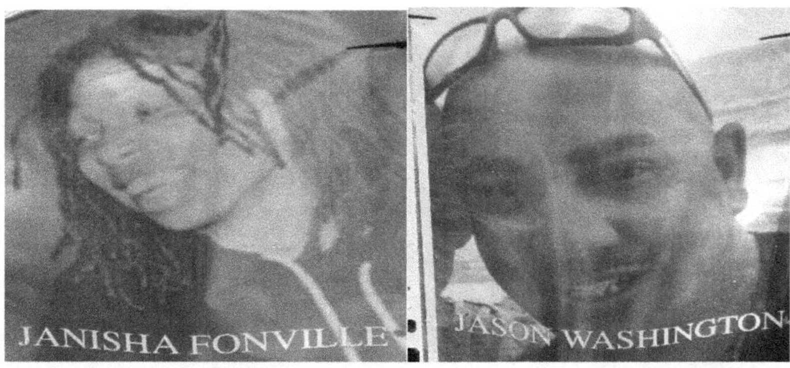

The Black Vote Photo – Say their Names – Janisha Fonville and Jason Washington.

The Black Vote Photo – Say their Names – Said Joquin and Samuel Hammond Jr.

"In 1965, the attempted march from Selma to Montgomery on March 7 was planned to dramatize to the state of Alabama and to the nation that people of color wanted to register to vote." **John Lewis**

"I don't think anybody has had more fruitful years on earth than John Lewis."

"For his nonviolent, peaceful protest methods, he was considered the Gandhi of America!" **Douglas Brinkley**

14. "TO DIE AND NOT BE FORGOTTEN" BY DR. FRED MONDERSON

The ancient Africans of the Nile Valley, Egypt and Nubia, were guided by a philosophic admonition, "To die and not be forgotten," for such an aspiration and realization was tantamount to not dying a second death, and so this helped to guide and dictate their moral and spiritual compass in directing their lives.

WHO SPEAKS FOR THE BLACK VOTE IN THE AGE OF TRUMP?

Consider this nation's population size, how many daily deaths and how many are remembered, discussed, and how fewer are discussed positively for their contribution to smoothen the road humanity, Americans, must tred. In retrospect, in contemporary times, among the names of Americans whose lives and contributions have been exemplar examples for Americans and ethnic groups in particular, African-Americans, have imprinted on American history, culture and iconography through the many who have been especially noteworthy. This has been true of the 20th and now the 21st Century

The names of Martin Luther King, Malcolm X, Marcus Garvey, Sonny Carson, Jitu Weusi, Rev. Lowery, John Lewis, Medgar Evers, Rev. Shillingsworth, Julian Bond, Fannie Lou Hamer, Queen Mother Moore, Madame C.J. Walker, Frederick Douglass, Mary McCloud-Bethune, and more have all been uttered in constructive remembrance for the mighty symbolism they represented during their time on earth, on the nation's and world's stage, and well after their passing. Of course, it's not simply the good that been said of a person but equally the bad. However, while the good may be quoted, even serving as shibboleth for future generations waging struggle, the bad often fades exposing the maliciousness of their intent and proponents as rightly so, only truth matters, survives and truly defines reality. Two examples particularly underscore this phenomenon especially with the passing of American icon John Lewis who transitioned on July 17, 2020.

The first instance was depicted on a CNN Program clip in praise of John Lewis' decently. Apparently, well into his many years as a Congressman from Georgia, an individual who, as a KKK member had attacked young Lewis in his days of creative yet peaceful protest. He appeared at Lewis' Washington Congressional Office to apologize and say he was sorry for his racist actions back then. The man of dignity, loving compassion and exemplary approach to the many persons he met, simply responded, "I forgive you!" Dismissing the serious damage, the man had inflicted on him and perhaps the KKK member's conscience began affecting his mental health for he looked in terrible shape, health-wise. This was a case of superb moral contrast. Significantly, however, John Lewis did not want to be burdened with the albatross of hate he could have entertained if he rejected the man's apology. Perhaps he had moved past the issue years ago. This is an iota of the decency and humanity that characterized this giant of a man, some called a titan, an American icon.

The second incident concerns John Lewis' passing on Friday, but President Donald Trump, after Tweeting some 41 times finally by 2:07 PM on Saturday, offered a terse recognition of the passing of the giant. Ok. So, Mr. Lewis questioned Mr. Trump's legitimacy as a president owing to the circumstances surrounding his election given so much was revealed about Russian interference, in the 2016 election. Significantly, and as is known, hardly anyone, even Mr. Trump's most ardent critics in the 2016

Republican Primary, had nothing to say and this underscored the courage this individual so praised in death had who dedicated his life to move the nation further to live out its creed, the American dream and its ideals, laws, institutions, cultural practices, etc. Mr. Lewis believed in this nation, believed in its possibilities and believed anyone can change, no matter how rabidly racist they are. Unfortunately, the president was too little a man to devote appropriate recognition and praise to Mr. Lewis, a Black champion. In response to a question by a reporter regarding Mr. Lewis' legacy, the President Trump knew nothing of it. Instead, he responded, he John Lewis, "Did not come to my Inauguration." How pathetic! Yet, Mr. Trump wants African-Americans to vote for him, when he disrespects Mr. Lewis as he did Elijah Cummings, Barack Obama, Maxine Walters, and so many others including the "Central Park Five" now declared the "Exonerated Five."

The Black Vote Photo – "People came to protest and this they did, in tumultuous numbers"

The Black Vote Photo – "Get Your Knee Off Our Necks," "Serve" and "Justice for George Floyd."

"If you ask me whether the election of Barack Obama is the fulfillment of Dr. King's dream, I say, 'No, it's just a down payment.' **John Lewis**

"If it hadn't been for that march across the Edmund Pettus Bridge on Bloody Sunday, there would be no Barack Obama as President of the United States of America." **John Lewis**

15. NO SELF-RESPECTING BLACK SHOULD VOTE FOR TRUMP BY DR. FRED MONDERSON

Congresswoman Ayanna Pressley told CNN's Jake Tapper, "John Lewis said Donald Trump is a racist." This is interesting for, being on the battlefield of social consciousness and reform, Mr. Lewis probably observed more expose on Trump than most and this led to his explosive realization and outspoken warning. Add this to the racist "Birther" charade and throw in his many statements of abuse, Mr. Lewis chose to stand up, speak his mind and "call the spade a spade." Even if observers overlooked the Pre-2016 election campaign, there has been a great deal as to why Donald Trump should not be re-elected but more important, hardly any Black person should vote for

Donald Trump's Re-election given he stands on the other side of decency where they stand. It is natural that people seeking answers to questions look to others who are more informed about the issue. General Mathis said Donald Trump had "no moral compass." James Clapper called Trump's behavior after publication of the tapes Bob Woodward made, "Egregious and reprehensible on several levels." Carl Bernstein said, he "allowed loss of life for his own political purposes" and that the tapes are "a recorded cover-up." Even further, while Trump can charm anyone, "The tapes are an ultimate smoking gun!" The above and following are persons and their ideas about the issues as concrete examples as to why the Black vote for Trump can be considered a waste given this group's moral and unending struggles to win, sustain and exercise the ballot, much more to give it to an avowed racist as Donald Trump, in many ways equated with George Wallace, Bull Connor and Sheriff Clarke, of Edmund Pettus Bridge fame. While Dan Coates, former DNI chief, believes "Putin has something on Trump," Abby Phillip explained "Trump creates his own reality."

The Black Vote Photo – "At Dr. King's Memorial" two images, two faces, same message.

The Black Vote Photo – Say their Names – Javier Ambler II and Jessica Williams.

The Black Vote Photo – Say their Names – Samuel Younge Jr. and Sandra Bland.

The Black Vote Photo – "Lovers Barack and Michelle Obama" and "Give Me Life, Justice, Prosperity" or "Give Me Death!"

In 1922 Caseley Hayford of Ghana, West Africa; opined the world had become so calculated, mechanical, materialist and lacking empathy, only the human nature of the African can save this globe from impending destruction. As part of that human nature, catalyst of conscience, the Black voter, because of the experience in America and the struggle to win the vote cultivated profound understanding of the concepts of good and evil; right and wrong; ethical and empathic; thereby recognizing useful and useless thoughts and actions. As such, in evaluation of the strengths and weaknesses of a candidate for the presidency, voters look for the values they admire before casting that cherished American privilege. This is no Rorschach Test as if some see Donald Trump as a racist and his base doesn't, then they are the same color and substance that he is made of. In fact, they support him unquestioned, his good and bad, no matter what! In similar fashion and more categorizing Donald Trump, in his bid to be Florida's Governor, Mr.

Gilliam said of the now Governor DeSantis, "I don't say he is a racist, the racists say he is a racist." Many of that right-wing community have "come out from under their rocks" and praised Donald Trump as one of theirs. Let's not forget, as with so many other negative associations Mr. Trump very conveniently denies knowledge of any such person as when he spewed, "I don't know David Duke!"

Now, in evaluating, whether to vote for Donald Trump, Blacks should determine whether he is worth their support; whether he lives up to the beliefs they hold and what do they have to lose in voting for Donald Trump. Trump is non-repentant, does not take responsibility for any negative result and he has demonstrated vindictive expressions. The Mother Emanuel Saints, on the other hand, forgave as did John Lewis and these are traits of the Black Voter. The case is closed! After all, look at the people he Trump appeals to, those who look up to him and whether or not Blacks would be comfortable in their company. It is not farfetched to imagine some in the group meeting with Mr. Trump may come with "ropes" and yet Trump may say, "I didn't see it." Let us not forget the imagery these people, "Tea Party" members especially, as they created the "black magic" characterization of Barack Obama on the outside, while Donald Trump worked his "white" "Birther magic" under cover of an aspiring candidacy.

1. Donald Trump's niece affirmed he is a racist, divisive, a weak leader, creating much damage to the

American nation and most important, fanning flames of division in divisive and racist rhetoric.

2. At his first **Inauguration**, Jesse Jackson thought Barack Obama "The best the civil right movement could muster." Much of the perhaps 82 percent of Blacks who voted for president were insulted and incensed by Donald Trump's "Birther" escapade, a smear campaign, he knew was false but it propelled his campaign, election and remained in effect well into his current administration. This action was approved by many who comprise the racist under and outer racist belly of America today. Some have called it hate but Mr. Clyburn was right when he said, "I don't mind if you hate me. I do mind when you disrespect me." "Hate could be natural, but disrespect means you think I am less than you." The same "Birther" hatred Trumps entertains for Barack Obama to this day. The question then for Mr. Cameron and your colleagues, "Have you ever considered the thought, Donald Trump only sees you from beneath his shoe sole like chewing gum. Imagine a "Tea Party" rabble thinking they were more than Barack Obama, twice elected President of the United States of America, a graduate of the most prestigious schools in America, a winner of the Noble Prize after serving as State and Federal Senator and well-liked throughout the world. He even scored in American polls as one of the greatest presidents of the United States. Meanwhile, these people's champion, Donald J. Trump is considered a liar, sore loser, weak leader, grabs women by the "Pussy," has been accused of sexual assault by some 16 American

women, even rape, has filed bankruptcy five times or more, was sued by the Federal Government for refusing to rent his properties to Blacks, don't want Black men counting his money in his failing casinos, has been sued untold number of times for improper business relations, paid "hush money" to "professional ladies," and thinks Mexicans are murders, rapists, sees an American Judge as insufficiently objective because he is of Mexican heritage, but another of Irish, Scottish or English descent could be objective in rendering a legal decision. Much of this seeming animosity has led to Donald Trump overturning significant accomplishments Mr. Obama was able to achieve. Who can say Mr. Obama's service and dedication was not in the best interest of his nation, the nation he inherited and worked his darnest to rescue? Now, all of a sudden, this racist white man, so full of hatred wants to overturn everything Obama did while claiming all of the foundations Mr. Obama laid, claiming them as his original creation. Yet, 190,000 Americans have died on his watch and Mr. Trump disdainfully boasts, "I don't take responsibility!" Early in February he knew the Virus was 5 times more deadly than the flu and that it was airborne. Yet he misled his own supporters holding mass rallies indoors with no mask and social distancing. He does take responsibility for the gains on the stock market Mr. Obama put in place. What hypocritical dishonesty. This is the man, without morals, wants Black people to vote for him to extend his pathetic administration and stewardship of the nation. Many of these particularly had some benefits for Blacks.

Today, while trying to rationalize his failure to inform the American people of the dangers of the Pandemic he confessed to Bob Woodward, he cited no need to panic. Yet, he pushed "panic controversy" with claims Blacks will overrun Suburbia; dangers of blacks on the warpath as in Kenosha, anarchist in Portland and so much more. What he refuses to say is, he abdicated his responsibility to the American people as their leader. Now, he has turned to Housing legislation Mr. Obama passed falsely claiming this will cause recipients to contaminate the Suburbs. Let's also remember, Michael Cohen says "Trump is a racist." He even cites Trump's sister and niece as well as several authors.

The Black Vote Photo – "Protesters **Say Her Name** going into and protesters coming out of the Martin Luther King Jr., Memorial."

WHO SPEAKS FOR THE BLACK VOTE IN THE AGE OF TRUMP?

The Black Vote Photo – "One big, happy family out to support the March on Washington, 8-28-2020."

The Black Vote – Photo – Say their Names – Jimmy Atchison and Jimmy Lee Jackson.

The Black Vote – Photo – Say their Names – Sandy Guardiola and Sharonda Coleman-Singleton.

The Black Vote Photo – "I Can't Breathe" – "The color of My Skin Should Not Put a Target on My Back!"

Strange these same accomplishments rescued the nation in the crisis Mr. Obama inherited. Thus, Mr. Trump has given the impression he is the number one and only American patriot. Stripped of all the malarkey, the only tangible reason assumed for Mr. Trump's actions is that Mr. Obama is a Black man.

3. Mr. Trump's assault on the Black population, whom he hopes will vote for him, is seen in this attack on the four Black Congresswomen he wants to "Go back to where you come from."

4. He labeled African nations, the heritage of African-Americans, as "shithole countries."

5. Mr. Trump believes Black Lives Matter is a symbol of hate but the KKK, Alt Right, Q-Anon and White Supremacists are "very fine people." The police do not kill these, they kill Blacks. The police disarm white killers but kill unarmed Blacks.

6. Trump disrespected Nelson Mandela, a great statesman the world admired for his principles.

7. Congresswoman Maxine Walters, long laboring in the vineyards of Congress seeking justice and equality for Blacks, was disrespected by Trump who, among other things, considered her a "Low IQ" person.

8. Journalists April Ryan and Abby Phillip and another in the White House Press Corps were ripe for his disparaging and disgusting abuse. Seems this misogynist has this thing against women, particularly

Black women. Michael Cohen said, "There was only one Black woman in the whole Trump Organization."

9. The pregnant wife of an American soldier killed in Niger, West Africa, Mrs. Johnson, was disrespected in her time of grief because of Trump's disrespect of and abuse targeting women, Black women, especially. Let's not forget his "Vagina grabbing" episode and the 16 women who accused him of sexual assault, and the one of rape.

10. While he called for the execution of the "Central Park Five" now determined to be the "Exonerated Five," in similar cases of wrongful conviction, the city would settle in financial compensation; but President Trump objected to this settlement to compensate for the wrong meted out to these young people he wanted killed.

11. John Bolton in his book, *In the Room Where it Happened*, revealed Mr. Trump's every action was concerned about his re-election and concerns about Black issues can only be construed falling within the realm of serving his own ends then being discarded as if viewed as chewing gum beneath his shoe sole. This is the man who wants the Black vote but when on stage he is not thinking Black, but white, right.

12. Mr. Trump's niece Mary Trump's new book, *Too Much and Never Enough* calls him a racist and anti-Semitic and that "He has a problem with Black people." She calls him "a psychologically deeply damaged person" who will get worse if he remains

"untreated," but he is "not interested in being treated."

Even more, he lacks leadership skills and is indeed a failure in this regard having been "played" by Putin, Xi, Kim, etc., all the while disrespecting America's strongest allies. In response to another book by Amarosa Manigault, he called her "Low life" "a dog." What crass language from "the man who would be king," I mean President, or has been and must not be again. Therefore, Trump must not be re-elected and of the few Blacks who were paid their "30 pieces of silver," shame is their lot until it's their turn to become a victim of "the child in a man's body."

13. Trump disrespected Congressman Elijah Cummings calling his district a "Rat infested hell hole." Anyone who stands up to him, he seeks to mercilessly tear down. This is dictatorial leadership, or effete leadership though still dictatorial is not the American way.

Let's face it, the man has no decency, a prime commodity African-Americans hold dear. His recent claims of voter fraud amidst the question whether he will accept the result of the election, nearly 90 days from now, means he intends to steal the election and not relinquish the office. This dog vomit he is forcing Republicans in the world's greatest deliberative body, insisting they eat this malarkey is part of the morsel he intends to feed the Black voter after he wins. The charlatans would ambush Biden but stay silent on the Trump volcano cascading across the

American landscape. Without question, the destruction of America will affect the Black voter.

Mr. Trump condemns mail-in ballots, a necessary requirement in view of the pandemic's potential impact on the many, especially the elderly, who would vote in person. That is, despite Mr. Trump and many of his people who vote absentee or mail-in ballot while he harps on "Voter fraud," itself a fraud; its voter suppression that has the most effect on any election and Mr. Trump and his supporters are principal in this voter suppression move.

"MLK, Jr. taught me how to say no to segregation, and I can hear him saying now... when you straighten up your back, no man can ride you. He said stand up straight and say no to racial discrimination." **John Lewis**

"When I was a student, I studied philosophy and religion. I talked about being patient. Some people say I was too hopeful, too optimistic, but you have to be optimistic just in keeping with the philosophy of non-violence." **John Lewis**

16. THE CHOSEN OF GOD: TRUMP AND JOHN LEWIS BY DR. FRED MONDERSON

"Many are called but few are chosen!" The claim to be chosen has been applied to both Donald Trump and John Lewis. However, who makes the realization and determination highlights the genuine nature and significance of such human interpretation of the workings and divine intent of intervening in human affairs is important. It's like "the saint" making himself a saint rather than the official mechanism. However, and as such, how the realization and intent is determined reflects the authentic nature of the message and how far-reaching the implications and utility of such an action reaches; who benefits and how do they respond.

The notion of "The Chosen One," "Chosen of God," was first amplified recently by Donald Trump after he bucked previous US presidents delicately handling of the Issue regarding Israel's capital location. After Mr. Trump forcefully recognized; all pandering for Jewish votes to aid his re-election campaign; on a roll, despite tremendous negativity associated with the man, his movement and administration undergirded in his vice-grip hold on the Republican Party, many questioned his decision. So, Mr. Trump boldly and publicly, in self-gratulation asserted, "I'm the Chosen One!" In this egotistical, self-proclaimed admonition, some commentators sought to paint the president, perhaps rightly so, with a broad, delusionary brush.

In his "Only I can" delusionary state and given his craving for foot-stools who willingly genuflect to kiss his ring, two particular sycophants, Energy Secretary Rick Perry, "The good-looking rascal," and Rudy Giuliani, "the president's lawyer and pitchman" quickly fell in line. It's not known if these two were instructed to so proclaim which is possible, or were free-lancing as curry-favoring, but Rudy, more publicly proclaimed the president was "The Chosen One" while Rick Perry seems to appear as whip cream with a cherry on top of the president's cake, gladly and essentially seemed to proclaim, "Yes boss, we sick." However, Trump and Giuliani both looked to the heavens muttering their delusionary falsity. Perhaps both men in fact looked to the heavens not for an affirmation of the statement but to dodge any potential thunderbolts thrown in the disgusting objection for such blasphemous intimation.

In his long delusionary state, Mr. Trump often boasted as a businessman, how wealthy he is. In America, persons don't care how wealthy you are, how you got your money, only that you have money. Jesus, in a land that proclaimed his divine nature, perhaps understanding how the rich get and keep their money, indicated their long-odds of winning the heavenly lottery. Then he chastised the "money changers" in the temple. Mr. Trump's presumptuousness, given his "bundles of baggage" would prove vexatious to saints, much more to any god-force sitting on a throne and observing in an audience hall in heaven. Mr. Trump has a problem, and the people who could meaningfully address it, Republicans in Congress, are too timid, busy cowering, fearful his vengeance could affect their chances of re-election, and so they stay silent. Yet, like the Carona-Virus pandemic, Mr. Trump's evil will one day evaporate.

The Black Vote Photo – "Early arrivals for the March on Washington – I am Good Trouble" and "Try Me – Black Lives Matter."

The Black Vote Photo – Say their Names – Jonathan Hart and Jonathan Sanders.

WHO SPEAKS FOR THE BLACK VOTE IN THE AGE OF TRUMP?

The Black Vote Photo – Say their Names – Solomon Mahlangu and Spencer McCain.

The Black Vote Photo – "The Message is clear – **Black Power**!"

The antithesis to Mr. Trump is, Representative John Robert Lewis, recently deceased. Here we have a man in love with and respected by everyone and who has dedicated his life, spending some 60 years getting into "Good Trouble," "Necessary Trouble." In his stellar career, he was arrested some 40 times as a civil rights activist and 5 times as a US Congressman, all in efforts to move the nation forward to become its most cherished idea of a more perfect union or as he has often said, "So the Revolution of 1776 could be finished." Unlike his antithesis, Mr. Lewis did not proclaim his divine mission, it was the people who saw this divine connection. While the movie **Ten Commandments**, perhaps shown more than any other, is fiction more than fact; yet, one episode seems to indicate the path and preparation to become "The chosen one." In the movie we see Moses leading his people before being "cleansed by the fructifying head of the desert;" while conversely in America, we see Mr. Lewis lead his people through the wilderness of hate, racial practices, take a stance against poor housing, inadequate health care, and inferior education. Most important; he, Mr. Lewis, remained steadfast against perennial victimization realized in conscious and unconscious bias in a system designed to be racially insensitive, brutal and oppressive, even with Biblical blessing. However, despite being a victim of such hateful vicissitudes, like the martyrs of Mother Emanuel Church, Mr. Lewis chose not to be burdened by retaliatory hate, but perennially uttered sentiments of love and forgiveness, while still drudging towards the mountaintop of goodness, mercy and empathy, as he admonished disciples, "Get in good trouble, necessary trouble."

WHO SPEAKS FOR THE BLACK VOTE IN THE AGE OF TRUMP?

While Mr. Lewis drank water to quench his thirst for justice and righteousness, Mr. Trump became intoxicated with power having drunk the rich man's wine, gorged on high quality Trump stakes, and the best of his hamburger meats. This, however, did not improve his standing, but actually demonstrated his "low life" behaviors and manifestations.

In a lengthy career of struggle towards mountaintop aspirations, equal justice, equitable social, education and economic opportunities and most important the right to vote and the unrelenting struggle against voter suppression, Mr. Lewis remained consistently courageous, his eyes steadfast on the prize, as evidence in his many proclamations, arrests and cleansing through the passage of struggle. In praising a life of exceptional struggle in the cleansing process while serving his fellow man, representative Bennie Thompson, Chairman of the House Homeland Security Committee praised Mr. Lewis for his "humility, commitment to justice and fair play, and his unrelenting efforts to make good out of evil." Among the hallmark behavior traits of Mr. Lewis, "the boy from Troy," was his courage, and laser-like focus on inherent injustice committed against Black, White, Brown, Native American, Gays, LGBT, Disabled, everyone, victimized in the American system. Very early, in protesting some such inequities, Mr. Lewis wrote President John Kennedy comparing the struggle of persons making five dollars per day with others making one hundred thousand dollars per year. As such, Mr. Lonnie

Bunch thought, "As a nation we were blest to have John Lewis as a citizen. He symbolized the best that America could be."

Those traits of concern for all buttressed in humility, forgiving nature and as a perennial optimist, enabled him to become a beloved figure in the nation's politics. Reverend William Barber called Mr. Lewis, "A man of the movement," because of his deep conviction. He pointed out, "Mr. Lewis went to Selma to join, not start a movement." Adding, after the murder of Jimmy Lee Jackson, Mr. Lewis embarked on his activist journey seeking jobs, justice and the right to truly and effectively cast the ballot. Thus, he joined the ranks of other greats as Jose Williams, Bayard Rustin, Dr. M.L. King, Asa Randolph, Reverend Lowery, Rev. Shillingsworth, all who "rushed to fill the jails in the civil right mission of dignity." He never gave up, he never gave in, always remaining positively committed to the quest and so influencing many along the way, one generation after another.

At his funeral in the Selma Memorial, one of Mr. Lewis' sisters praised the American titan by repeating one of his popular refrains, "See Something, Say Something, Do Something." Another brother recounted, upon Mr. Lewis election to the Congress, as he sat in the balcony and Mr. Lewis knew where he was seated, in the **Inauguration Ceremony**, the new Congressman looked up at his brother and gave him a thumbs up. Later he asked the sibling, "What were you thinking when you gave me the thumbs-up?" John responded, "This was a long way from the cotton fields of Alabama."

Sentiments such as these and more, propel the journey seeking justice, the right to register and vote, being paid a living wage, challenging the inequities of share-cropper peonage and systematic diminishing of land ownership, against public policy that benefits the many not the few, advocating for meaningful health care, to be entitled to appropriate sick leave for workers, rent relief, and most important restoration of the Voting Rights Act protections. It is a tragedy that this legislation has sat on Mitch McConnell's desk for some 2,700 days as CR Bill 1904. These and more are some of Mr. Lewis' good works achieved as a result of his "good trouble," "necessary trouble," activism. Such are the commitments, successes and failures, that cause the people to proclaim, indeed this was a man of God, "the Chosen One." This is not a self-congratulatory fabrication Trump and his stooges banter about, but a genuine expression by people's realization and acclamation; a true and honest "pay back," for a life of commitment and personal sacrifice in America's best interest.

After all, god who sees the hearts of all men does not pour good wine into filthy vessels. God does not choose liars, "pussy grabbers," racists, proponents of racial divisiveness, the vicissitudes who demonstrate poor leadership and whose only concern is to be reelected and unconcerned as in the deaths of more than nearly 200,000 Americans brought about by a devastating pandemic where leaderless, true or not, no plan is offered. What is bad, Trump lied, he hid the truth and now he wants to rationalize his behavior after the fact. Shame!

First of all, sinners such as Rudy Giuliana would not be entrusted with the ability or inspiration to declare Donald Trump as "the chosen one." After all, he is Donald Trump's lawyer and as such, it's tremendously far-fetched to think he would not lie for si client. Thus, looking up is out of fear not out of inspiration or for confirmation.

The Black Vote Photo – "Legalize Being Black" and "Justice, Fairness, Liberty, Equality, Freedom, Inclusion, Opportunity and Equal."

WHO SPEAKS FOR THE BLACK VOTE IN THE AGE OF TRUMP?

The Black Vote Photo – Say their Names – Jonie Pilar Block and Jordan Edwards.

The Black Vote Photo – Say their Names – Stephen Lawrence and Stephon Clark.

It can be argued, nature is a god and has visited the pandemic pestilence on America because of Mr.

Trump's callousness and insensitivity. More so, it's because of his incompetence, his lying nature, concealment, fooling the nation and especially his base, now bearing the brunt of the pestilence. How sad, one man in red now confesses "I don't care if I get it" shows his willingness, "To die for Trump!" Now, while the American people can't wait "To see Mr. Trump's darkness evaporate," they long for the light Mr. Lewis radiated. Thus, while Rudy and Rick, and even so perpetrated by Donald do falsely proclaim, themselves perpetrators and victim of a "con man" operation falsely parroting "The Chosen One" mantra; only the people are the ones who can rightly make such a designation and they are the only ones who can and did honestly affirm, "John Lewis is the Chosen One."

Bakar Sellers, an author and commentator, recounting Lewis' career and admonition reminded, "freedom is not free. It requires action to secure it." And so, he equated Mr. Lewis with Dr. M.L. King, Marion Barry, Julian Bond, Stokely Carmichael (Kwame Ture), Ella Baker, Fannie Lou Hamer, Jose Williams and Rev. Joseph Lowery, among many others.

Today, the cry is, "We don't want ceremony" though Mr. Lewis will lay in state in the Alabama Capital in Montgomery and the Nation's Rotunda in Congress. For the nation to truly honor this noble soul and iconic son of this nation, Mitch McConnell should approve and the president sign the bill to restore the Voting Rights Act's provision recently scuttled by the Supreme Court. Then again, it may be a cold day in his domain for Mr. Trump to honor John Lewis who objected to his presidency owing to Russian interference in 2016 and having been out there for some 60 years must have accumulated knowledge of Donald Trump's racist actions to call him a racist.

Too often Malcolm X reminded, "History is a good teacher." When Marcus Garvey was victimized and falsely sent to Atlanta Federal Prison, on the way, he raised his manacled hands and admonished, "You have caged the lion but the cubs are running free out there. Look for me in the whirlwind." Because of John Lewis' work and commitment, to seek justice and equality, humility and forgiving nature, his courageousness, as god has molded him into a "Chosen" vessel, his steadfastness in search of his destiny has been an example in crafting cubs.

This writer once met Representative John Lewis at Rep. Major Owens' funeral in Brooklyn, New York, where he recounted, "You can tell a Morehouse man, but you can't tell him anything." There he also praised his **Alma Mata** and his sorority *Phi Beta Sigma*. There I came up-close to a man who stood for democracy, liberty, freedom, possessing courage and honesty in his dealings, traits that appeal to "young people who are the lifeblood of the movement" among whom John Lewis walked so proudly. "Along that path, he came from poverty to lead the nation." This "moral conscience of the Congress," who came from humble beginning to achieve greatness, has "finally gone home to the bosom of god." That is an acclamation and reward for being "The chosen one." Say no more.

How wonderful is it, while we mourn and protest the murder of George Floyd, we also celebrate and acclaim a great hero of the black pantheon, an illumination of a "thousand points of light," one of the best examples of the goodness of the African spirit, John Robert Lewis, a great and fearless American statesman and citizen.

The Black Vote Photo – "Biden/Harris for America" and "Vote 2020" – "We Will Not go Back – "March for Justice."

"We are one people; we are only family. And when we finally accept these truths, then we will be able to fulfill Dr. King's dream to build a beloved community, a nation, and a world at peace with itself." **John Lewis**

WHO SPEAKS FOR THE BLACK VOTE IN THE AGE OF TRUMP?

"I was so inspired by Dr. King that in 1956, with some of my brothers and sisters and first cousins - I was only 16 years old - we went down to the public library trying to check out some books, and we were told by the librarian that the library was for whites only and not for colors. It was a public library." **John Lewis**

"John Lewis will be considered a founding father of a fairer, more inclusive, better America." **Barack Obama**

17. ITS JOE'S SHOW BY DR. FRED MONDERSON

In a Viet Nam movie, somewhere down in the Aisha Valley, a hill was the issue of serious contention producing untold American casualties. The Black Combat Medic who treated many of his comrades finally succumbed to battlefield injuries. As he was being ferried out by helicopter, his parting words to his remaining comrades were, "Take the Damn Hill." Today, that enemy on the "Hill" is Donald Trump and his Republican enablers who cannot, out of fear, "see evil, hear evil or speak evil." In one *Fast and Furious* episode, after the hero had crashed his car into the villain, he called him the "P" not "Protester" word.

Charlatan opponents of Joe Biden may wimp and pontificate but not only do they not have any stake in the outcome of the 2020 National election, its whether or not they can deliver the votes in question. Such pontificators stand, nevertheless, to gain ratings but still, after all is finished, they move on to the next delectably exciting media frenzy, all the while showing gains in one way or another. Joe Biden, however, is a horse of a different color. His boats are burnt; its win or bust! He must win or lose everything given he has tried to become president unsuccessfully a number of times as part of a lengthy career in public service. As such, the notion of being "held hostage" to pick a Black woman as his running mate is not a credible or realistic option. After all, he is forced to make the right choice, put together the best combination to be successful in this important quest, and bears full responsibility for the outcome. He has served in the position of Vice-President and knows what it takes to fulfill that mission. Again, Joe Biden has everything to lose and "charlatan's talk is cheap." This latter seems to equate with a crying Kanye West who announced his intention to run for President and whom some believe was a "sixth wheel" to the trojan horse coach seemingly implanted to siphon off Black votes from the viable Biden effort.

Equally too, falsity of word is, young people don't vote or Joe Biden doesn't seem sufficiently charismatic to drive them to the polls to contribute their part to the overall effort to bring the needed change. First, Joe Biden is not the problem. Donald Trump is! Even more important, Joe Biden is not an end; he is a means to an end. The end is removal of Donald Trump from the Presidency as well as retiring his aimless minions, such as Mitch McConnell and other Republican enablers of Donald Trump whose action will crowd the future of the same young people. From a lifetime of activist struggle with an eye on the total political landscape, accumulated knowledge forms opinion of fact. In this regard, John Lewis pointed out, "Donald Trump is a racist" and he supports, winks at racists and retweets racist tropes. With such a mindset and in the frenzy, he generates, there seems no place for Black voters whose support he courts and craves and as we see, are not in any of his photo-ops. As Malcolm X reminded, "The nation is so evenly divided, the Black vote is crucial; it determines who go to the White House and who go to the Dog House." We must send Donald Trump to the "Dog House."

Photographs tell an enormous story. As we see with Senate Majority Leader Mitch McConnell, so with Donald Trump, only white men are seen behind them in any photo-op. Such an image will not characterize Joe Biden. There will be Black influence in Joe

Biden's decision-making team including the Campaign's Co-Chairman and "that Sanders Lady," as a spokeswoman. This person seeks and speaks truth not unlike spokespersons who parrot "alternative facts" and are everyday caught in lies to protect Donald Trump.

When persons as former President Barack Obama and Representative James Clyburn, who helped Biden diminish the competition in the South Carolina Primary, vouch for him, then we will see Black men and women in any Biden Photo-op and in meaningful positions in his new Administration.

The Black Vote Photo – "We March, y'all mad. We sit Down, y'all mad. We Speak Up, y'all mad. We Die, Y'all Silent, "**BLACK LIVES MATTER**" and "Sandra Bland, Stephon Clark, Atatiana Jefferson, Philando Castile, Mike Brow, Alton Sterling, Tamir Rice, Jordan Davis, Freddie Gray, Amaud Arbery, Breonna Taylor, Eric Garner."

The Black Vote Photo – Say their Names – Joyce Quaweay and Joshua Dariandre Ruffin.

The Black Vote Photo – Say their Names – Steve Biko and Susie Jackson.

The Black Vote Photo – "**God is Dope**" and "**Alpha Phi Alpha**" "The Immortals say: 'Get Your Knee Off Our Necks.'"

The young people must come to see Donald Trump as not simply a threat to the nation at this time, but he is a threat to their future and their children's future. Remember, the conservative judges he has and will continue to appoint will be a force to reckon with for decades to come. He has appointed judges throughout the federal judiciary system. He has appointed two justices, Brett Kavanaugh and Justice Gorsuch to the Supreme Court. Mitch McConnell often boasted about the more than two hundred federal judges he and President Trump have appointed so far. Tumultuous young and Black turnout can and must bring this to a halt.

Now, in the case of Justice Ruth Bader-Ginsburg, an octogenarian; ill, yet holding on to her seat awaiting Donald Trump's replacement. Otherwise, if she lets go, as Mitch has already boasted, "I will appoint him right away!" Then Donald Trump will be afforded the opportunity to appoint another conservative judge to the Supreme Court and this will for a long time tilt the delicate balance now comprising the Court. Thus, the issue is not necessarily Joe Biden but the sum total of who and what Donald Trump represents; equally, persons who approve of or are not critical of his racist, divisive, obnoxious behavior and effete leadership, are guilty and must be removed. Great Blacks as Barack Obama, James Clyburn, Susan Rice, Senator Tammie Duckworth, Senator Kamala Harris and a whole lot more chose to come together to combat the plague Trump represents, threatens and perpetuates. Therefore, good and righteous Americans must vote November in unprecedented numbers for Joe Biden as the needed bulldozer that must remove Trump.

James Clyburn, a man of extraordinary respect, long active in the belly of the beast, dealt with the issue of "a Black woman" running-mate for Joe Biden. His response was simple, "A Black woman on the ticket is a plus, not a must."

To the charlatan's claim Blacks have been voting Democrat for the longest and have nothing to show for it. This ignorant trope is dangerous for it, nonetheless is a confluence of a Russian hoax and a Republican voter suppression talking point and strategy, even if these proponents feign calculated innocence, which, in fact, is ignorance. After all, there are some 60 Black Democrats in Congress and 1 "symbolic" Black Republican. The late Representative Major Owens once remarked regarding the Black Caucus in Congress: "People ask what do we (The Black Caucus) do in Congress. It is not the legislation that we pass. It is the legislation we block in conjunction, compromise and association with colleagues. So much frivolous legislation is proposed on the House floor, it is important we be there to stop or slow it down." That John Lewis' Voting Rights Act legislation has been languishing on Mitch McConnell's desk in the Senate for a total of some 2700 days, is a strong indication of this pervasive maliciousness. The Black vote is significant for they elected the first African-American president; Obama paid Black farmers, whose money was languishing in Washington; today Obama knowledge and presence is "keeping Blacks in the game!" Alas, it is not altogether that Barack Obama is Black that Donald Trump hates him. We have seen past that "Birther falsity." It is more the fact that "Obama has been there and done that" and "knows a thing or two" is a principal reason Donald Trump seeks to undo much of his legacy.

Let's be reminded, for more than a century, Black have been victims of voter suppression efforts, and if observers and analysts only count from the Obama years, Republicans in charge of statehouses, through legal and extra-legal means have prioritized orchestrated removal of Black voters from the rolls. This has been on-going and it falls under the voter fraud claim and no Republican, certainly none of note, has called this claim unfounded or unjust. Many have observed, this notion of voter fraud has been a consistent, though false, claim of Donald

Trump. After all, the man is a lying machine, so what can you believe comes out of his mouth but lies.

Since, according to John Lewis, regarding Trump's fraudulent election with Russian assistance, one prominent Black female Professor shouted on TV, "Voter fraud, Voter fraud, Voter fraud, it's a lie. Voter fraud does not influence an election, voter suppression does."

Most people think the reason for Donald Trump's slide in the polls is the Carona-virus, the resulting economic downturn, as well as his divisive and racist chatter. This may be so. However, given more lies than truth comes out of his mouth, Americans don't know what to say or think, when Trump speaks. He downplayed and lied about the Carona-Virus' impact for too long, knowing as in early February it was deadly, airborne and many times more lethal than the flu; yet, he deflected and readily defended statues of Confederate traitors who perpetuated and defended slavery, killing Americans and posing the deadliest threat to the American system. Mr. Trump did, however, rightly point out, "If Democrats vote in tumultuous numbers Republicans can't win." Hence, the Post Office sabotage and fraudulent voter fraud claim and the truth about voter suppression efforts are not being seriously examined as fraudulent and put to rest. Let us again, not forget, this demagogue falsity extended to charges of "fake news," vindictive behaviors, insensitivity towards the plight of many and trump only seems interested in promoting what is good for Donald Trump and his interests. That is why, in countering Trump's undermining of a fundamental tenet of American democracy, as John Lewis has long admonished, "We must vote like we have never voted before." As such, Mitch McConnell and the Republican Party hypocrites will never renew the Voting Rights Act sitting on the Majority Leader's desk for nearly 2700 days. That is again why, we must vote like never before to send Mitch and his boys packing.

At this point in time, Joe Biden is the only one to lead the charge of the Black Brigade and his choice of a running mate is an issue now settled and can be discussed later. Personally, I thought he would name Susan Rice or senator Kamal Harris as the best choice! Rice is smart, familiar with the issues, has been our United Nations' Ambassador and National Security Adviser to President Obama. In that role she has worked closely with Vice-President Biden and he of all persons know of her qualification, experience and capabilities in this critical time in the nation's history. Senator Harris has been elected as Da and attorney General of California, a statewide position and so can bring that generally Democratic state into Biden's column.

Therefore, this is the time when, quoting President John Kennedy, "Ask not what your country can do for you, ask what you can do for your country!" What Americans can do is send a message to Donald Trump: "Hurry up and do what you can constructively to help clean up the messy situation you created, clean out your desk, and call the moving vans." "Goodbye Mr. Trump," come January 20, 2021, 12: Noon! Then, either the FBI or men in white jackets will greet the then "fake president!"

The Black Vote Photo – "People of Quality do not fear Equality" and "Get Your Knee Off Our Necks."

The Black Vote Photo – "The **Black Immortals**" at the "**Black Lives Last Supper**!"

The Black Vote Photo – Say their Names – Junior Prosper and Justus Howell.

The Black Vote Photo – Say their Names – Tameka Lashay Simpson and Tamir Rice.

WHO SPEAKS FOR THE BLACK VOTE IN THE AGE OF TRUMP?

The Black Vote Photo – “Black Nutrition Facts” and “Black Lives Matter!”

When I was 15 years old and in the tenth grade, I heard of Martin Luther King, Jr. Three years later, when I was 18, I met Dr. King and we became friends. Two years after that I became very involved in the civil rights movement. I was in college at that time. As I got more and more involved, I saw politics as a means of bringing about change.” **John Lewis**

“There are still forces in America that want to divide us along racial lines, religious lines, sex, class. But we’ve come too far; we’ve made too much progress to stop or to pull back. We must go forward. And I believe we will get there.” **John Lewis**

18. IS CHARLEMANE THE 2020 VERSION OF THE 2016 PUFFY? BY DR. FRED MONDERSON

Let's face it. There will be two candidates in the 2020 Presidential election. These are, the Democratic nominee Joe Biden and President Donald Trump, the Republican, seeking re-election. The former Vice-President Joe Biden, appearing on "Charlemagne da God's" morning radio show *The Breakfast Club* made a blunder stating essentially (1) Black voters either vote for me or Donald Trump. (2) If you vote for Donald Trump, then you are not Black, meaning, "I have stood with black people for the longest, served as Vice-President to Barack Obama and received the great bulk of Black votes in the now aborted Presidential Primary." This writer did not hear the Biden interview, but did observe Charlemagne on Erin Burnett's **Out-Front** program on CNN.

There, the anchor replayed part of the Biden interview, particularly the controversial statement then queried Charlemagne. He did respond essentially, "His listeners raised questions, as he identified the need for a Black woman as Senator Harris and Stacy Abrams and that Blacks have been voting for white men and did not get anything in return" and *ad nauseum.* Regarding the Vice-President, "I'm not interested in what Biden has done in the past, I'm interested in what he will do in the future." One wonders if he considered what Trump has done so far and what he will do in the future? Persons like Charlemagne clap with one hand and even "high five" himself with that same one hand! The problem in this statement is that Charlemagne has taken it to be the final arbiter of the Black vote. People who understand the issues, believe James Clyburn, Hakeem Jeffries and Maxine Walters among others who should run with this. More important, however, while Blacks need to appear monolithic in this issue, instead there has been a fissure and confusion that confuses most Blacks who are not sophisticated in this respect.

The comparison of Charlemagne with Puffy is they both have an audience and both have made forays into political decisions that affect Black people and the Black vote, resulting in negative consequences.

Unknowingly, Charlemagne may have thrown Donald Trump a political bone and in process confused or offered doubts to the Black voter. In the case of Puffy, on the other hand, I'm confused. Now, here's a young man; a multi, multi-millionaire. Fact is, he started out as Sean Combs, then changed his name to Puff Daddy, Puffy, P. Diddy, Diddy, and now Puffy. The only problem is, who is who? Nevertheless, the problem with Puffy became evident when in late 2015 on Al Sharpton's show; he, in commenting on the upcoming 2016 election featuring the democratic candidate, Hillary Clinton, Mr. Combs advised, "Hold the Vote" which certainly alarmed Sharpton. Many who heard his voice, "held the vote," and did not vote. This certainly helped Trump to win and so we have this mess.

In January 2016, Rev. Sharpton held a legislative forum in Washington and Representative James Clyburn, in addressing the group, warned, "This is the most consequential election of our time." Many Blacks held back and Trump won, not necessarily because of this but it certainly had impact. Charlatanism is a form of voter suppression and young and Black voters must keep their eyes on the prize, the issues and looming threat posed by complacency. Donald Trump's lies, misinformation, divisive politics, racist banter and even the "30 pieces of silver" he can dole out to people influenced by his version of the truth must not rule the day. As a liar, who knows if any promises he makes will be kept? I'm reminded of one of the *Robin Hood* movies starring Russel Crowe. King Philip of France began an invasion threatening England and King John, a usurper, implored the Barons to aid the cause in interest of saving the country from the foreign forces. As soon as he got rid of the threat, he rescinded his promise and then attacked Locksley.

Given Donald Trump is an "I don't know the guy" type of person, once re-elected, we can expect he will go back on his word. Remember, "Vote for me and I will set you free;" then "Rap on Brother!"

"The March on Washington was a March for Jobs and Freedom. There are still too many people who are unemployed or underemployed in America - they're black, white, Latino, Native American and Asian American." **John Lewis**

"We need Comprehensive Immigration Reform, Dr. King wouldn't be pleased at all to know that there are millions of people living in the Shadow, Living in fear in places like Georgia and Alabama." **John Lewis**

19. SIMPLE WORDS, POWERFUL MEANINGS BY DR. FRED MONDERSON

President Obama said, "Yes, We can!" and it came to pass. Nike Posted, "Just do It." A follow-up mantra read, "I did it!"

During the **Harlem Renaissance** of the late teens and early twenties of the Twentieth Century, amidst terrorist intimidation, racism and lynchings especially in the American South, Claude McKay wrote his famous poem, "If We Must Die." The significance of this poem has been a potent **Battle Hymn**, then as well as even today.

The Black Vote Photo – "Black Lives Matter" and "Stop the Murders" – They Can't Breathe!"

The Black Vote Photo – "Mandate National Reporting of Use of Force Incidents!"

The Black Vote Photo – Say their Names – Kajuan Raye and Kalief Browder.

The Black Vote Photo – Say their Names – Tanisha Anderson and Tavis Crane.

The Black Vote Photo – **BLM** – "The Ancestors Approve!" "No Justice No Peace."

The Equal Justice Initiative of Montgomery, Alabama, led by a southern legal eagle chronicled some 4040-lynchings of Blacks in some eight southern states. These horrifying and ghastly unspeakable terrorist acts of lynchings were done under the noses of law enforcement officials yet no one was brought to justice despite the public spectacles that drew thousands of joy-filled spectators comprised of men, women and children who gorged on the agony of the unspeakable acts of lynchings and mutilations. A few years ago, a CBS Public Affairs Program, investigating a murder in the south where the perpetrator was still alive and only the victim's family was speaking up, the narrator referred to some "100-unsolved civil rights murders" that still baffles the FBI.

The recent murder of the young Black jogger Amaud Arbery in a Georgia town that his father described as a "modern-day lynching" and state authorities are investigating as a possible hate crime was not only ghastly but demonstrates an unintended message. Whether intentionally or not, but realizing the inevitability of his impending death, Mr. Arbery chose to live Claude McKay's resounding shibboleth, "If We Must Die," "Dying, But Fighting Back!" a reality he lived to the end. In fact, McKay's Poems is as follows:

"If We Must Die, let it not be like hogs
Hunted and penned in an inglorious spot,
While round us bark the mad and hungry dogs,
Making their mock at our accursed lot.

If we must die, O let us nobly die
So that our precious blood may not be shed

In vain; then even the monsters we defy
Shall be constrained to honor us though dead!

O kinsmen! We must meet the common foe!
Though far outnumbered let us show us brave,
And for t heir thousand blows deal one death-blow!
What though before us lie the open grave?
Like men we'll face the murderous, cowardly pack,
Pressed to the wall, dying, but fighting back!

And, as the video demonstrates, Mr. Amaud Arbery fought to the end!

In his urgent call to open the economy, in one example, Mr. Trump told his followers, "Liberate Michigan!" As a result, many supporters appeared at the State Capital armed, threatening, calling for the lynching, even beheading of the governor, etc. What is interesting, in so many areas particularly the South, Trump's supporters are now feeling the brunt of the Corona-Virus sting because he lied to them and the American people. No less significant, in another setting, a newsflash showed at a protest when Trump's armed intimidators appeared, they were met by heavily armed young Black men who seemed to say, essentially: "We know you will kill us, so we're going down fighting like Mr. Arbery. Too long have you killed our people, nothing has been done and all Americans have the right to bear arms and defend themselves."

WHO SPEAKS FOR THE BLACK VOTE IN THE AGE OF TRUMP?

"We need someone who will stand up and speak up and speak out for the people who need help, for people who are being discriminated against. And it doesn't matter whether they are black or white, Latino, Asian or Native American, whether they are straight or gay, Muslim, Christian, or Jews. **John** Lewis

"I have met every president since President Kennedy. And I think Barack Obama must be listed as one of the best. This young man has been so inspiring - not just to people in America but to people all around the world." **John Lewis**

20. THE NEW, NEW NORMAL BY DR. FRED MONDERSON

After the terrorist assault on September 11, 2001, Vice President Dick Chaney laid it down, we have now entered the "New Normal." Now with COVID-

19, the Coronavirus that appeared in December 2019, hence its name, has been so devastating, we have entered another "New Normal." In the case of the 9/11 "New Normal," a number of anti-terrorist measures were put in place; Citizens were called upon to be more vigilant. Signs appeared that read, "If you see something, say something." Law enforcement officers began appearing with security dogs able to detect devices that may cause bodily harm. In places of transportation, particularly at airports, security screening trying to be extremely effective has created lengthy processing times but citizens have come to recognize and understand such measures are necessary for safety purposes.

In public buildings such as courts and government offices, security apparatus was installed and this too has contributed to more time in processing, but again, citizens seek to cooperate. Because terrorists have used vehicles as weapons of mass destruction targeting civic and others buildings of high human occupancy, innovative concrete devices now surround such important structures, providing an artistic flair, but most important contributing to success in thwarting attempts of terrorist intent. Even on airplanes, not only have pilot compartments been more properly secured, armed air marshals are assigned as passengers on flights. These measures and more were instituted to combat the potential of further terrorist attacks that defined the "New Normal."

WHO SPEAKS FOR THE BLACK VOTE IN THE AGE OF TRUMP?

True, the anticipated challenges were and are human behavior driven and as for example, as in a game of chess such measures can be anticipated. With the "New, New Normal," everything is different.

The devastation of the Carona-virus Pandemic, the American economy hemorrhaging tremendously, Donald Trump spewing falsity and divisive racist and incendiary messages that undergird his lack of or poor leadership, even threatening to delay the election in November are examples of the "New, New Normal." The handling of the Carona-virus Pandemic that has claimed 190,000 American lives; the protest in the streets; government's poor reaction to citizen outrage forces many observers across the globe to conclude the stature, moral fiber of America has plummeted. That is the "New, New Normal and unless Donald Trump is removed from" the Presidency, it's no longer "Sky's the limit, but basement is the reality."

The Black Vote Photo – "Black Kids Matter, Peace Not War, Black Lives Matter" "**Vote Him Out** – "**Protect Black Trans Women**!"

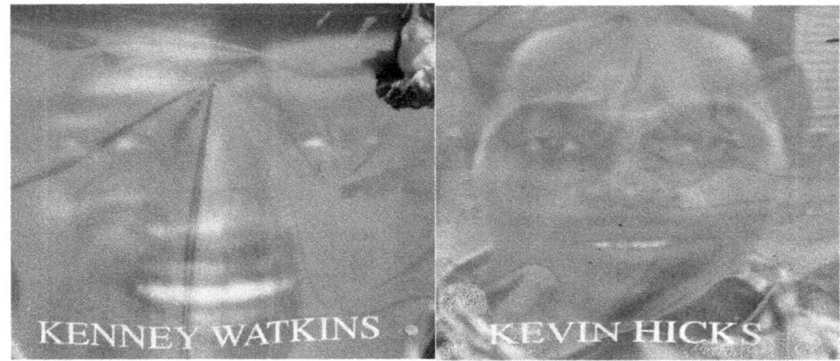

The Black Vote Photo – Say their Names – Kenney Watkins and Kevin Hicks.

The Black Vote Photo – Say their Names – Terrell Johnson and Thamsan Qaminele.

The Black Vote Photo – "We're not trying to start a race war; we're trying to end one" – "Justice for those Abuse, Manipulated and Murdered by the System.

"The civil rights movement was based on faith. Many of us who were participants in this movement saw our involvement as an extension of our faith. We saw ourselves doing the work of the Almighty. Segregation and racial discrimination were not in keeping with our faith, so we had to do something." **John Lewis**

"I think President Barack Obama has been a good president" **John Lewis**

21. KAMALA – "AIN'T I A WOMAN TOO?" BY DR. FRED MONDERSON

On hundred years after women won the right to vote, Senator Kamala Harris has been chosen to be former

Vice-President Joe Biden's running mate for the Vice-Presidency role for President in the upcoming 2020 National election on November 3rd. Instantly, after being nominated, President Donald John Trump attacked Senator Harris in the most vile and racist manner calling her "nasty," "angry," and a "mad woman." If she ultimately becomes President, he feels "It's an insult to America." Imagine this creep who can't admit his actions has been an insult to America. Such language and much of Mr. Trump's divisive actions are clearly racist and demeaning to Black citizens, especially but to all Americans in general. Except, perhaps his base." Now, a sort of decorum is expected of the President of the United States who speaks for the American people which essentially says to the world, "Since I speak for the American people this is how they express their views." In response, the world would purportedly respond, "If this is so, then Mr. Trump's 'base,' his supporters, his 'suburban housewives,' accepts 22,000 lies that he has spoken; that they take pride in his public boast of "grabbing women by their private parts;" does not find reprehensible that some 17 women have accused him of rape and sexual abuse, in addition of paying females for sex while his wife is pregnant and lying about it; they have no objection to his attacks on 4 Black, female, legislators telling them to go back to where they came from, even though three were born here and the forth a naturalized citizen; that Mr. Trump disrespected Congresswoman Maxine Walters, reporters April Ryan, Abby Phillip and Jasmine Wright. Therefore, in support of Mr. Trump, his base "owns" much of his exposed "nasty" behaviors.

While there is political challenge, not only has Mr. Trump orchestrated a systematic assault against Kamala Harris as a woman, but we may recall, Megyn Kelly, House Speaker Nancy Pelosi, Michigan Governor Whitmer, even the grieving and pregnant Mrs. Johnson whose husband was killed on a military mission in Niger, West Africa. He leveled a low blow against Mrs. Khan standing silently beside her husband, a gold star family whose son Captain Khan died in Iraq serving in America's Army Mr. Trump weaseled out of and is now its Commander-In-Chief.

Today, amidst one of his many racist tropes, Mr. Trump boasted "Suburban housewives will vote for me," as if "white women" in the Suburbs will overlook Donald Trump's misogyny and vote for him regardless. In the waning days of slavery, Sojourner Truth, recognizing the inhumanity meted out to the enslaved African woman, viz., the lash, rape, emotional and sexual abuse, even lynching and intimidation as one of several unspeakable acts committed against them including other forms of killings and so she appealed to abolitionist women, "Am I not a woman, too!" Essentially then, as now "Am I not a woman like you, capable of doing what no man can do." That is, produce a child. We must remember, even in the Civil Rights struggles to secure the vote, Malcolm X often reminded of "The brutes with their knees on women" accompanied by dogs pulverizing American citizens seeking the privilege and protections of constitutional guarantees. The same women whose sons and husbands were deployed to defend this great nation then as now, in fact since the beginning of the nation. Thus, Mr. Trump's arrogant bombast paints "suburban white women" as supporting Trump's racist banter, untold numbers in sustained street protest in support of Black Lives Matter, against his thousands of lies, falsity and misinformation, effete leadership that seemingly meets "Suburban women's" approval.

Therefore, women, irrespective of race must send a stern message to Mr. Trump, his enablers and the world, they are distant from such detestable behaviors and will express their disapproval on November 3rd.

Recently, during the President's Impeachment, the House Team appeared somewhat "forceful" in presenting their case. Then, Chief Justice John Roberts reminded all, they are "members of the world's greatest deliberative body." Today, a brute has planted his knee on the stomach of one of their members, a Senator, both State and Local Attorney General, and very few Republican Senators have had little to say whether regarding the "adjectives" Trump uses or the false "Birther" trope he falsely peddles on Twitter and at the microphone that should be about Corona-Virus and his failed leadership that has allowed some 190,000 American deaths; yet, this outstanding American is, in this "ogre's" eye ineligible to be Vice President because she may not be born in the United States. She was born in California but the nation is familiar with this liar's "Birther" games.

The historical record has shown, while the Japanese Secret Service, the Nazi Movement and Mussolini's Fascists were on their destructive path, supporters abounded. In their later crashing defeat, many denied association with the movements they wholeheartedly supported. In similar fashion, an angry mother nature has brought America to its knees, as a result of the Covid-19 Carona-Virus Pandemic. And in historical comparison, Trump's pathetic psychological, rational, humanistic imbalance will tumble and many aboard that "ship of fools" will ultimately scamper as "rats who desert a sinking vessel." Unfortunately, Donald Trump has tied his fate, a cement block, unto the feet of the "suburban housewife." However, perhaps like the one prisoner of "Plato's Cave," some of these women may experience the prescient realization President Trump's "Domestic abuse of Senator Harris" is no different from the experiences of someone they know of suffering from similar disrespect by a barbarian who could not acknowledge and appreciate the intelligence of an educated, thinking, rational, creatively critical woman of substance who refused to be considered and treated as a piece of flesh by an uncouth misogynist.

The Black Vote Photo – "Haitians stand with **Black Lives Matter**."

The Black Vote Photo – Haitian Revolutionaries stand with "**Black Lives Matter**!"

The Black Vote Photo – Say their Names – Kisha Michaell and Kiwi Herring.

The Black Vote Photo – Say their Names – Tilly Gulley and Tony McDade

The Black Vote Photo – "Biden 2020 – BLM" and "Enough!" "**Educated and Black**!

And so, in sisterhood, naturally in support of Senator Kamala Harris, the Democratic candidate to be Vice President, women must send a clear message to Donald Trump, "We reject not simply your brutal treatment of all women, Black, Brown, White, Yellow, whatever, but the crass and reprehensible manner of your behavior in general" and so, "Don't take our vote for granted!"

In memory of 100 years of women's struggle to secure the right to vote, for equal treatment, pay and all forms equality, we must elevate not degrade women, no matter race, religion or social status and this should be the message going forward for brutes such as Donald Trump and his pathetic enablers.

Mr. Trump's treatment of Senator Harris, a historic pick, a fighter who challenges a substantial barrier, seeking to break the glass ceiling, in which her candidacy equally shines a light to transform the status and condition of women in general, is an appalling exercise in failed leadership.

The Black Vote Photo – More of the outraged masses coming out of the Martin Luther King Memorial, and again, add Conscious Redirecting of the Black Dollar and see what happens.

The Black Vote Photo – "7 Shots in the BACK!!!" and "I Have a Dream (MLK) 1963 August 28, 2020" "Black Lives Matter "

The Black Vote Photo – "My Roots" and **Black Lives Matter**!"

"Selma helped make it possible for hundreds and thousands of people in the South to become registered voters and encouraged people all across America to become participants in a democratic process." **John Lewis**

"We should be creative, and we should accommodate the needs of every community to open up the democratic process. We should make it easy and accessible for every citizen to participate." **John Lewis**

22. STAND STILL ... BY DR. FRED MONDERSON

"Stand still and witness the salvation of the Lord!"

Word has it that the Trump Administration had considered revoking former President Barack Obama's Security Clearance, but this ridiculous and possibly vindictive idea was shelved. This act began the breech of his oath of office to serve as a model of justice and equality for all Americans. Nevertheless, such a decision comes after Donald Trump's championing the "Birther falsity" he "red herringed" that grew legs and ultimately projected him to the United States Presidency. Meanwhile, in his capacity as President during his tenure, Mr. Obama was fully-engaged at the well-known critical junction of the nation's history.

The Obama Administration was unique in a number of ways but principally as the first African-American President of the nation. Number 44 challenged failing norm practices and created economic and financial policies that placed the nation's economic structure on a sound footing. He rescued banks and "Wall Street;" the auto and housing industry as well as state and local governments shortcomings were given a tremendous "shot in the arm;" while remaining committed to the war on terror, Iraq and Afghanistan and much more. Now, while the Obama Presidency created a reservoir of pride and dignity for the Black experience at home and much goodwill to the American cause abroad, all were because of the man's elegance of mind and nobility of spirit. This and more are reasons people love Obama.

As all this unfolded, Sunday after Sunday and intervening week-days, Saintly grand-mothers and grand-fathers, their sons and daughters and grand-children gathered in church houses to pray for Barack Obama; a man on a divine mission to save America tottering on the brink of financial and economic ruin; joblessness; housing collapse; and managing the nation's involvement in global conflict creatively. President Obama, with his head down began turning the battleship of state away from the threatening waters of doom and he did it successfully. Yet, challenge, he had to contend with the masquerading evil and racist implications of "I intend to make Barack Obama a one-term President" Mitch McConnel; disrespectfully shocking "Birther King"

Donald Trump consistently asking for birth certificate, while as Cohen admitted, he hid his sister revealed he was a "C" student.

But they were not alone. After Obama orchestrated the Affordable Care Act, Senator DeMint called for his "Waterloo;" Michele Bachmann accused him of running "a gangster government" in a city where, the FBI is head-quartered along with some 22 other American security agencies including the CIA, NSA, Etc. All the while, Senator Grassley declared Obama "stupid;" Rick Santorum accused him of "poisoning the well;" "Lipstick on a Pig" Sarah Palin had charged he was "palling around with terrorists." Nevertheless, in the general society because of his policies, people were returning to work, banks began lending again, the auto industry regained its market share, housing starts picked up, then Obama deployed his "primary weapon" Michelle Obama on the world stage in which she "floored the Queen," "wow" the Germans; "disarmed" the French while earning the moniker "Mighty Michelle."

Still, out of jealousy, full of racial animus, the "Tea Party" gathered in nefarious fashion; Militias paraded threateningly under false pretexts; all the while Ted Nugent sang their chorus of "The Nigger in the White House." Yet, undaunted, the grand-mothers prayed and prayed for President Obama and oh, what a glorious transference of religious and spiritual nourishment and empowerment such efforts were for their hero on a mission. Nevertheless, Obama continued to swim among sharks, barracudas and piranhas but remained wary of their bite. After all, he admitted, "Politics is a contact sport." Sadly, on their knees in conversation with their god, Dylan Roof entered that Holy Sanctuary in resplendent KKK, Confederate and Nazi regalia then killed 9 in "Mother Emanuel." No less alarming, the surviving Saints, similarly as Jesus on the Cross said to the Centurion, "We forgive you. We don't want to be burdened with your hatred."

And so, as the wheels of truth, justice and righteousness - Ma'at, rolled on, President Obama "fought back to be re-elected." This come-back in favorability was against the coordinated assaults, disrespect, the climate of racist animus and deceit generated as a result of McConnell's failed quest; the coordinated strategy of Ed Meese aided by some 22 CEO's of Republican NGOs, who all mobilized against the ACA they maliciously misnamed "Obamacare." Joe Wilson could not resist and so injected his "You lie," as the President of the United States delivered the State of the Union message in the Hall to the House of Congress. And the Elders prayed on for Obama and the nation, generating tons of spiritual, ethical and emotional strength and goodwill the oppressor could not counter.

Then the "Lord of Hosts" decided to intervene! Still, baffled, he began weighing the requests of Evangelicals even while noticing Blacks on their knees, enjoining to bring good into the world. These oppressed persons had good reason to engage their god, especially after the deaths of Trayvon Martin, Michael Brown, Eric Garner, Gurley, Tamir Rice and more as a climate of questionable public and private behavior unfolded. But who could question divine design and intent? Still, the black-white divide began turning into a chasm.

The Black Vote Photo – "Black boys became criminalized. I was in constant dread for their lives because they were targets Everywhere. They still are." **Toni Morrison**

The Black Vote Photo – Well- dressed Black Men at the "March on Washington" August 28, 2920.

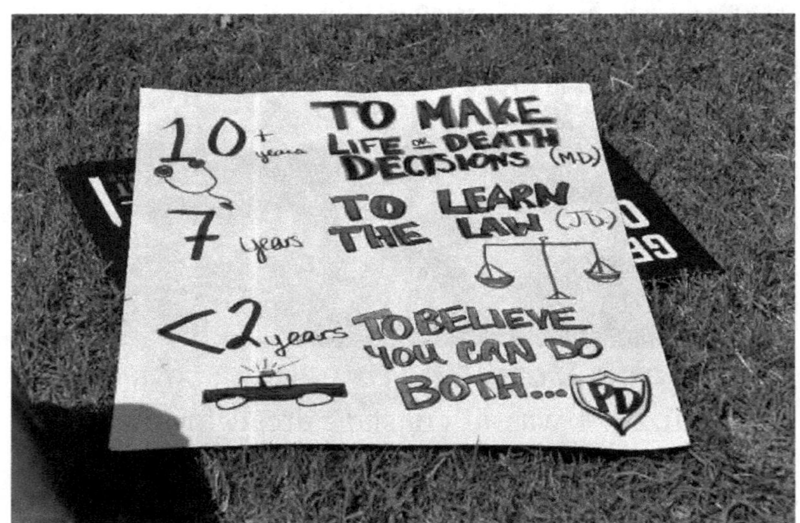

The Black Vote Photo – "10 + years to Make Life or Death Decisions; 7 years to Learn the Law; Less than 2 years to Believe you can do both."

The Black Vote Photo – Say their Names – Korryn Gaines and Kwame Jones.

The Black Vote Photo – Say their Names – Tony Robinson Jr. and Toussant Diamon Sims.

The Black Vote Photo – **"Black Lives Matter to GOD and Me!"**

The Black Vote Photo – They keep coming for "Justice and Commitment" now add boycotted Black Dollars and see how quickly the wheels of justice move.

WHO SPEAKS FOR THE BLACK VOTE IN THE AGE OF TRUMP?

Who knows, perhaps the divine decided to chastise America and so allowed Donald Trump access to the Presidency in the cosmic realization, "You only get one shot." In the resulting tumultuous celebratory exuberance from under every rock came an emissary. The glitter of "new penny jewelry" blinded everyone. Moving quick under promise of hiring "the best people" President Trump began rescinding Obama's Executive Orders, engaging corporate entities on the economic and financial pedestals Obama created, while Wall Street began its historic climb. Republicans were elated and touted each success. As they saw it, Mr. Trump boasted then, "Only I can do it!" Concurrently, his administration enabled some "30 best men" who were accused, convicted, abused the public trust and many ended up in prison. So much for his choice of good men or was it they did as he in abusing the public trust?

And so, the base, which actually means "bottom" loved their President. It was as if relieved of "Black rule," the "Great White Hope" had arrived. And so, this "Bull in the China House" began running rough shod over everyone, insulting the media, touting "fake news" claims, and even evoking Obama at every turn trying to sully his legacy as he genuflected to Putin and his Russians. Through it all the Saints remained on their knees praying, a fallen angel will not consume all.

Meanwhile, given "Absolute power corrupts absolutely," Donald Goliath began trampling across the social and political landscape of the nation.

Sowing confusion, denying everything, lying like no other, still he must have had a sense the Avenging David was on the way.

As myriad of events began unfolding the questionable Trey Gowdy chose to "run" and "fight" in another arena; "Stupid" Grassley, discombobulated and speechless, to this day, remains dumb-founded; Wishy-Washy Senator Graham is proving a master of zig-zag; and only Bob Corker stood and delivered! While Mitch McConnell and Speaker Paul Ryan, in face of nearly 200,000 Donald Trump lies, misstatements, plus insults, racist rants and more, both failed to do the manly thing as the people's representative John Brennan has indicated, Mr. Trump is "drunk with power." And so, the behemoth spread, like the librarian in **BLADE**, spewing darkness across the American moral and ethical landscape while spewing political rants that continue to divide the nation. Many of the President's "best people" fell short and were removed from office or ran afoul of the law. For example, Michael Cohen – pleaded guilty – 8 counts; Paul Manafort – guilty – 8 counts; Michael Flynn – guilty – lying to the FBI; George Papadopoulos – guilty – lying to the FBI; Scott Pruitt – 14 investigations into his tenure; Tom Price – HHC boss -fired; Steve Bannon forced out; Jeff Sessions – Recluse - Omarosa Manigault-Newman – turned traitor. Then there is Rob Porter, fired for spousal abuse. Strange that every time one of these things happen, the President describe these as "good people." As David Axelrod exclaimed, Mr. Trump is "offensive to the truth."

WHO SPEAKS FOR THE BLACK VOTE IN THE AGE OF TRUMP?

Even as the Special Counsel Robert Muller sifted through the myriad of evidence, he successfully brought 191 criminal charges against 35 defendants while securing 5 guilty pleas. It's a generally philosophic belief, "one man can become a majority if his truths are immutable." In light of the 2016 election claims of Russian interference, Trump making nice with Russia, one man "called out" the President and in viewing the overt evidence pronounced "the king is naked." Naturally he braced for the backlash but his many years of service to the nation made John Brennan and so many others, immune to Trump's water pistol. Perhaps that water falling to earth germinated the prayers of the Saints on their knees which began the budding opposition to injustice and tarnishing of the American ideal. Perhaps their prayers will continue to be answered. After all, those saintly people who identified with the Black man in the White House, had suffered so much from the insults, humiliation, even racist climate directed toward President Obama, they prayed even more.

"Whom the gods wish to destroy they first make mad." In this regard, Martin Luther King reminded, "The arc of the moral universe is long but it bends towards justice." In the streets of New York, many learn, "What goes around comes around." Perhaps the conviction of Mr. Manafort and Mr. Cohen were part of the "Big Payback" answer to prayers for the years of Obama persecution, insults to Black women, sports personalities, Mexicans and other Latinos. Mr.

Trump has shown no concern for diversity, a pillar in the strength of America. Let's not forget the "Central Park 5" whom he tellingly disparaged, which all seem to indicate for Mr. Trumps, while the "Cows are not there yet," the "Chickens have certainly come back." Thus, in comparing Obama and Trump, we see Midday and Midnight. You go figure, who's who.

President Trump has his many plates full; he had many fires burning as an enormous cloud settled across the American skies. This has unsettled him terribly. This is a man in crisis. His base chose to be oblivious to such developments because in his utter contempt for the rule of law, he kept insisting, "Don't believe what you read. Don't believe what you see. That is not what is happening." In his "alternative universe" of evasions and untruths the continued echoed repeats of "No collusion" is not correct. In that "out of this world place," his Adviser Kelly Ann Conway offered "Alternative facts" and his attorney Rudy Giuliani insisted, "Truth is not truth." Such pronouncements are naturally unrealistic. In this regard, the award-winning journalist Carl Burnstein speaks of the "sewer seeping up from the White House swamp." Nevertheless, like lemmings in Trump's "alternative universe," his supporters, seem clueless and bent on following him over the cliff. What is the truth, however, is that after President Trump suspended John Brennan's Security Clearance, he then published an additional "enemies list" of ten names whose clearance he was considering suspending?

WHO SPEAKS FOR THE BLACK VOTE IN THE AGE OF TRUMP?

For a man who secured several military deferrals due to "bone spurs" and who is now Commander-In-Chief of the nation's armed forces and whose "enemies list" may have given more than 300 years of service defending this nation, the insult was unbearable. So, Admiral William McRaven (Retired), who oversaw the raid to eviscerate Osama bin Laden considered Trump's description of the press as the "Enemy of the people," as the "greatest threat to our democracy." In response, he wrote, "Suspend my clearance so I can stand next to John Brennan." Then 15 intelligence personnel penned a letter in support of Brennan and the Admiral. These were joined by 60 others and again by another 175 American service patriots, who essentially told the President as did Admiral McRaven "you have embarrassed us before our children, humiliated us on the world stage, and worst of all, divided us as a nation."

The Black Vote – "Warning – Educated and Black!"

The Black Vote Photo – "Peace Comes After Justice" – "Staying silent in times of Injustice is Privilege."

The Black Vote Photo – Say their Names – Lajuana Philips and Lamar Smith.

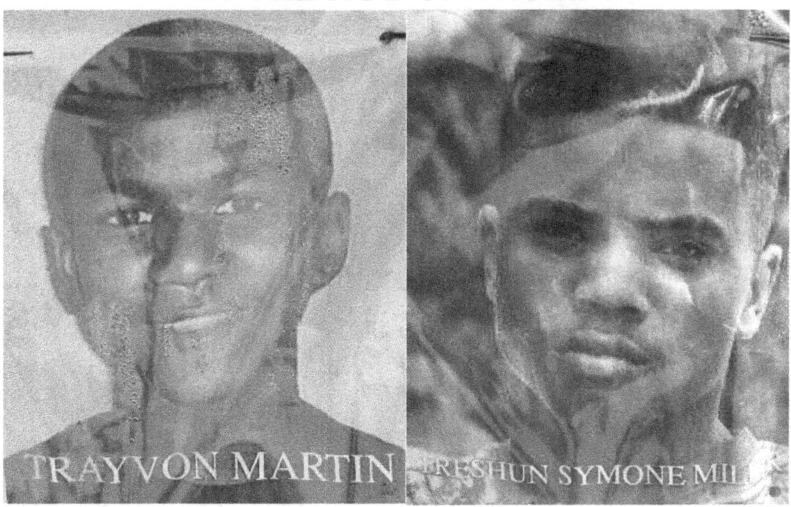

The Black Vote Photo – Say their Names – Trayvon Martin and Freshun Symone Mills.

The Black Vote Photo – "If you are silent about your pain, they'll kill you and say you enjoyed it" and "Noboyd's Free Until Everybody is Free."

Naturally, in their jubilation of false triumph, his base never saw and still does not see this rebuke coming. Today, despite Mr. Trump's taped conversation with Bob Woodward describing the Carona-Virus as five times worse than the Flu, while not telling his people about this secret, they love him even more. Some think it is a hoax and see no need to wear protecting face coverings nor do social distancing. In fact, they fail to see the big picture facing a worried Trump who has been obfuscating in text. Still, Trump faced the specter of Muller, McGhan, Omarosa, Cohen, Manafort, Gates, Stormy Daniels, Karen McDougal, Vladimir Putin, Kim Jung Un, China, Iran, and an unleashed Brennan, Clapper, Hayden, and much, much more. The man has "20 lives." But, as Mr. Friedman has indicated, "Trump's Teflon is mud, and if you throw mud on him, it does not matter. Still, h He must certainly be worried. Significantly, this man of spite, bigotry, racism and homophobia, in the words of Omarosa, "Trump has met his match." Matching this, many have argued, "corruption is the feature of the Trump Administration."

The Black Vote Photo – "Kneel with me, not on me – "You must never be Fearful about What you are doing when it is Right" **Rosa Parks**.

However, whatever may be said of Omarosa, she has brought home the bacon! We heard about, even speculated about Donald Trump but now she has recorded goods on him in the form of video, recordings, pictures, emails. Of course, this was same as Bob Woodward's collection. Nevertheless, added to this, Donald Jr. is also in trouble for lying, even meeting with an American adversary's representative. In all this, Paris Dennard, Ben Carson, DA Cameron, Kanye West, the Cleveland Pastor, Mark Burns, Kelly-Ann Conway and all the trump apologists, loyalists, his "best people," many of whom were fired for criminal and unethical activities, are now saddled with and must deny "Trump's sh-t don't stink." Fact is, these people are so far in, they're in the Perfume room.

The real question is will Donald Senior and Junior share the same cell as Muller tried to do and even as Michael Cohen advises, "Mr. Trump resign and let Mike Pence pardon you or face criminal charges if you stay on. Meanwhile, as the Saints continue praying, they "Stand to Witness the Salvation of the Lord" in all its magnanimous retribution.

"If you're not hopeful and optimistic, then you just give up. You have to take the long hard look and just believe that if you're consistent, you will succeed." John Lewis

"I want to see young people in America feel the spirit of the 1960s and find a way to get in the way. To find a way to get in trouble. Good trouble, necessary trouble." **John Lewis**

23. VOTE OR DIE! Well... By Dr. Fred Monderson

The next general election in November 2020 is tremendously important for a number of equally important reasons; particularly national and state, whether combatting voter apathy or expressing concern about the "new normal," national trend or the President's performance in terms of his response to the pandemic, Bob Woodward's new book Rage, revelations of his niece's and Mr. Bolton's topped by Michael Cohen's Disloyalty: A Memorial, all recounting the preponderance of filth now in captivity of the White House. So, people must understand the importance of voting to bring about change. As someone who has voted in every election since 1972, I was dismayed by a comment made around the time of the primary last September. Asked whether he was going to vote this individual responded "No! I don't like the politics of Albany!" As such then, a critique of his behavior as well as voter apathy in general is very apropos.

Some people need to be reminded the struggle for the right to vote, particularly by blacks, in America has been a long, difficult and challenging experience fraught with deception, bloodletting and disappointment. Still, while the disenfranchised won the right to vote, there has been and still continues a movement to disfranchise particularly Black segments of the voting constituency. Hence, any form of "voluntary disfranchisement" should not be condoned.

The Civil War (1860-1865) resulted in the "Civil War Amendments." 13th, 14th, and 15th that conferred freedom, citizenship and the right to vote on the freed African-American, but also on citizens, native born or naturalized. This really meant males for women were still excluded. To exercise that first ballot experiment African-Americans travelled a rocky road to the voting booth. They were subjected to voting restrictions through literacy tests, fraught with problems; poll taxes that didn't always apply; property taxes even if persons didn't own property; disqualification at the poll; deceptive signs that misdirected voters away from the polls; and the "grandfather clause" that trapped first time voters.

Don't get me started with the Ku Klux Klan, Knights of the White Camelia; Brown Shirts, all terrorists by today's definition who intimidated and killed blacks through lynching, tar and feather and other forms of threats and disfigurement. Finally, when Black people persevered, at great personal risk and elected their representatives these officials had to battle prejudice and discrimination on the way to and from the legislative chamber. Perhaps that is why today Representatives are immune from police action on way to the Chamber.

This experiment collapsed with the end of Reconstruction and those the voting rights were designed to help lost a great deal in the 100 years that ultimately gave birth to the Civil Right Movement. After tremendous struggle at great personal cost, the 1964 Civil Rights Act gave Americans the 1965 Civil Rights Act with the mandatory renewal clause every 25 years. The irony of this latter reality is that though African-Americans are among the most loyal Americans, they are subject to this discriminating and dehumanizing experience. That is why John Lewis fought so hard to get the bill pass that now languishes on Mitch Mc Connell's desk for more than 2700 days. Let's face it. Germans, Italians, even the British, French as well as Japanese and Russian-Americans, people who have killed and threatened America and Americans in wars, are not subject to this legal handicap. Nevertheless, despite all of this power of the ballot to elect African-Americans and be influential in other races it's a reality that cannot be wasted.

WHO SPEAKS FOR THE BLACK VOTE IN THE AGE OF TRUMP?

In South Africa, the great majority had been prevented from voting and when given the opportunity that historic vote pictured extra-long lines that vindicated Nelson Mandela's ordeal and the worldwide struggle to free him and South Africa.

In this country, the audacity of Barack Obama to run for and win the presidency was a tremendous opportunity for African-Americans, young voters and other minorities and people in general to cast that historic vote.

On the national level, many people have criticized President Obama for not delivering on the change he promised, expecting a magic wand fix what ails America. Conceptually speaking, the belief is that he would have built up a "skyscraper of change" that would have addressed unemployment, housing, financial and economic reform opportunities, energy, education, internal improvements, health care, while waging two wars in Iraq and Afghanistan and fending terrorist threats, with Somali pirates and all, even while battling Republicans in and out of Congress. These many challenges and more the President faced against a recalcitrant scorched earth obstructionist policy driven Republican party with one goal in mind, **Stop Obama at all costs**! What was not evident up to now is that the Republicans had built a "sub-valley" size hole that the President had to fill before he could reach ground level. That is like "filling the substructure, constructing the structure to build the superstructure of clean energy, better and a more robust education system and science endeavor, added with economic, financial and capital reform and improvements in housing, health care and all forms of job creation designed to improve the condition of all Americans but particularly those persons who believe in the vision of President Obama Some understood the nature of the opposition committed themselves to vote in unprecedented numbers to ensure his agenda gets the recognition and protection it deserved.

The Black Vote Photo – "The Commitment 2020 March" – "I'm a Fan of the Black Woman – 08-28-2020 – I Was There" and "The Commitment 2020 March" – "I'm a Fan of the Black Man – 08-28-2020 – I Was There."

The Black Vote Photo – Say their Names – Laquan McDonald and Laronda Sweatt.

The Black Vote Photo – Say their Names – Tyre King and Tywanza Sanders.

The Black Vote Photo – "Justice Too Long Delayed, Is Justice Denied" and "When You See Something that is not Right, Not Fair, Not Just, Do Something, Get in Trouble, Good Trouble, Necessary Trouble."

"What I try to tell young people is that if you come together with a mission, and its grounded with love and a sense of community, you can make the impossible possible." **John Lewis**

"When you make mistakes, when you're wrong, you should admit you're wrong and ask people to forgive you." **John Lewis**

24. HONORING JOHN LEWIS, AGAIN BY DR. FRED MONDERSON

The Commitment "March on Washington" of August 28, 2020 occurred on the 57th anniversary of the original 1963 "March on Washington" in which Dr. Martin Luther King gave his famous "I have a Dream Speech. This original and historic gathering was not about a **Dream** but prevailing conditions of racism, high unemployment, treatment of poor people and rampant institutional racism that particularly galvanized the civil rights movement. Sadly, African-Americans paid a heavy price for the bold and courageous actions that forced the nation to recognize its failure to live up to its own ideals. Today, such circumstances are practically mirrored but there are even more deep-seated issues that brought out the current gathering.

Foremost in his belief in justice, the ability to bring about change and the potential goodness of the American people and nation, Mr. Lewis never stopped echoing words of wisdom and comfort that helped make this nation great.

"More marchers will come now!"

"We shall Overcome!"

"It is in our power to remake this country until it reflects our ideals."

"They liberated all of Us!"

"America was built by people like John Lewis."

"The testing of o ur faith produced perseverance."

"We have to be vigilant against the darkness of this country's history."

"The most powerful tool we have which is the right to vote."

"Republicans have pushed and passed a flood of laws designed to make voting hard."

"Republican actions are an attack on Democratic freedoms."

Jamila Thompson – "If you are of age, for the love of God, please vote!"

"John Lewis possessed traits that were human and divine."

"The work continues. The fight continues."

Sheila O'Brien – Niece of John Lewis – "My uncle was larger than life. He was a fountain of hope, courage, bravery, and sheer humanitarianism."

John Lewis "spoke of those who could not speak, and he walked for those who could not walk! He was a champion for those who could not fight."

Barack Obama – "John Lewis was a man of pure joy and unbreakable perseverance."

"A forceful vision of a free democratic country is a constant work in progress."

"As a participant of Freedom Rides, he struggled to change, minds, hearts, nations, the world."

Mr. Lewis was subjected to constant violence and daily indignities, but he would never give in, nor give out."

Josea Williams – John Lewis was full of purpose. God put perseverance in him.

John Lewis struggled against state sponsored violence.

The Black Vote Photo – "My Life Matters" and "I Can't Breathe" – "Black Lives Matter!"

The Black Vote Photo – "Our Demand is Simple – Stop Killing Us" and "Free-ish Since 1865."

The Black Vote Photo – Say their Names – Lashanda Anderson and Latasha Nicole Walton.

The Black Vote Photo – Say their Names – Virgil Lamar Ware and Victor White III.

The Black Vote Photo – "**BLACK LIVES MATTER!"** They sure do! – And "Get Your Knee Off Our Necks."

"We must be headlights not taillights." **John Lewis**

"I say to people today, 'You must be prepared if you believe in something. If you believe in something, you have to go for it. As individuals, we may not live to see the end.'" **John Lewis**

25. "THE RUSSIAN THING" BY DR. FRED MONDERSON

The more Donald Trump opens his mouth or not, the more the American people truly sees what "an absolute fool" he is. He told Lester Holt, the TV Anchor, "This Russian thing" is why he fired James, Comey, former FBI Director. As his mountain of lies grows, his Russian involvement expands as much in the same smelly manner as if guided by some unseen hand. His cultist base, even Republicans seeming devoid of testicular fortitude, from evidence, seem oblivious to the putrid odor of the Russian thing, even as it poses a devastating threat to American interests. It is interesting, all the hoopla about Republicans not stepping up and criticizing Donald Trump out of fear of their re-election, its more probably the racist bombast he spouts that is a true reflection of their views. In fairness, this does not apply to all Republicans, in and out of government, but those that can make a difference remain silent.

Very early, as the Muller Investigation unfolded raising questions of Russian collusion, whether Russia had anything on Donald Trump became a talking point that got much buzz. Some folks wondered whether the Russians could blackmail Donald Trump at America's expense. The Russians are white and Donald Trump made it quite clear, he too is white. So, why **Black** mail him?

Early evidence indicated, Donald Trump Jr., boasted Russian monies bankrolled many Trump projects. There has also been talk, Russian oligarchs purchased property from Mr. Trump at steep prices which seemed suspiciously like money laundering. Talking heads looked at his Beauty Pageant in Moscow and wondered if he was taped in amorous encounter with ladies reminiscent of the James Bond movie **From Russia With Love** as seems to be one tool in Russia's arsenal. Then the Muller Report dropped and though Muller could not conclusively prove "collusion" because John Bolton did not spill his beans early enough, the Report did list some 10 instances of Trump obstructing justice. Falsely, Donald Trump prattled, "No Collusion, No Obstruction, folks!"

Now, this is the guy who does not "take responsibility," that is, only when its favorable to him and so he claimed Muller exonerated him. So, let's not forget Bill Barr's Obstruction of Justice efforts on behalf of Donald Trump in which many in the Justice business were highly critical of the Attorney General for his efforts as "Trump's Attorney."

The Russian debacle hit the fan when, after US Intelligence, one of the best in the world, revealed Russian interference in the 2016 Presidential election. Muller called it "massive interference." However, standing beside Vladimir Putin in Helsinki, Mr. Trump responded to a reporter's question, saying essentially, "Putin told me he did not do it." This embarrassment, undercutting of American intelligence and interest, on the world stage besides, America's staunchest enemy, was a cause for national concern and the question became why? Equally, Mr. Coates, the Director of National Intelligence, on a radio show was surprisingly told, 'Do you know, President Trump intends to invite Putin to the oval Office?' Mr. Coates may have had an 'accident.' Today, nearly four years later, after the Bob Woodward revelation, General Mattis thought Donald Trump "unfit for office" and again, Mr. Coates expressed, whether, as he thought, "The Russians may have something on Trump." Thus, many began thinking of him as "A Manchurian Candidate."

Persons as Carl Bernstein reminded all, during the 2016 campaign, Donald Trump publicly stated, "Russia, if you're listening, I hope you can find Clinton's e-mails?" Apparently, they went searching and did find them. Then Trump praised Wiki-Leaks when they revealed hacked data damaging to Clinton. Recent revelations indicate Roger Stone was in touch with Wiki-Leaks before and after they published leaked information gotten from Russia. Strange, nearly at the end of his tenure of office, there is no available information about Donald Trump's diplomatic discussions with Putin, Kizlyak, or other Russian government official even of what transpired in the Oval Office.

The Black Vote Photo — "Black Incarcerated Lives Matter; Black Drug Dealer Lives Matter; Black Undocumented Lives Matter." "Black Lives Matter; Drug Dealers Lives Matter; Black Undocumented Lives Matter" – And, "We Believe Black Lives Matter; No Human is Illegal; Love is Love; Women's Rights are Human Rights; Science is Real; Injustice Anywhere is a Threat to Justice Everywhere; Respect Women of Color."

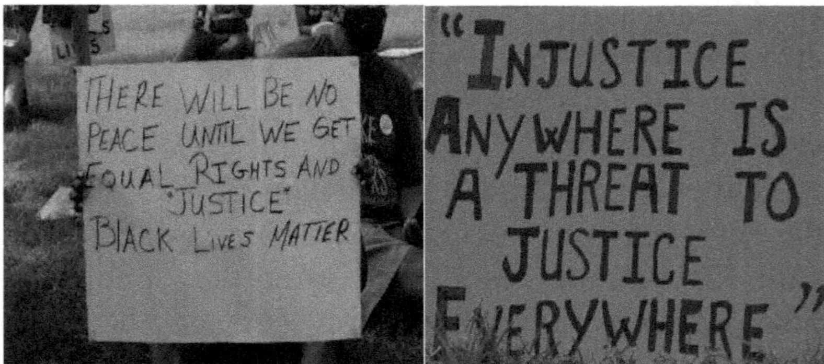

The Black Vote Photo – "There will be No Peace Until We Get Equal Rights and Justice" – "Black Lives Matter" and "Injustice Anywhere is a Threat to Justice Everywhere."

The Black Vote – Photo – Say their Names –Marielle Franco and Marlon Lewis.

The Black Vote Photo – Say their Names – Vuyisile Mini and Walter Scott.

The Black Vote Photo – "I'm Black Every Month" and "Black Lives Matter."

The Black Vote Photo – "Marchers in Jubilation" for "Commitment" as they exit Martin Luther King Memorial and "Black Lives Matter."

WHO SPEAKS FOR THE BLACK VOTE IN THE AGE OF TRUMP?

The Black Vote Photo – “Together We Stand Against Racism” and “Brothers of Influence Fighting for Justice.”

“I thought I was going to die a few times. On the Freedom Ride in the year 1961, when I was beaten at the Greyhound bus station in Montgomery, I thought I was going to die. On March 7th, 1965, when I was hit in the head with a night stick by a State Trooper at the foot of the Edmund Pettus Bridge, I thought I was going to die. I thought I saw death, but nothing can make me question the philosophy of non-violence.” **John Lewis**

“We have come a long way in America because of Martin Luther King, Jr. He led a disciplined, nonviolent revolution under the rule of law, a revolution of values, a revolution of ideas. We’ve come a long way, but we still have a distance to go before all of our citizens embrace the idea of a truly interracial democracy, what I like to call the Beloved Community, a nation at peace with itself.” **John Lewis**

26. BLACKS AT THE REPUBLICAN NATIONAL CONVENTION BY DR. FRED MONDERSON

The role of Black speakers at the recently concluded Republican national convention was designed for one purpose only. That is, explain why President Trump is not a racist and therefore Blacks should vote for this individual seeking re-election to the Office of the Presidency. In a foolish display, these individuals were seeking to pin angelic wings on a moving target and so they kept getting it wrong and shamefully must own Trump's ridiculousness. We must understand one true strategy of voter suppression is to get Black "leaders" to vouch for white candidates. However, unquestionably, if John Lewis says "Donald Trump is a racist" he has more credibility than a bunch of Blacks who appear as buffoons as the opposite of their contention keeps unfolding in real time, right after their praise of a man whose photo-ops do not even involve these testifiers! How sad, Donald Trump's recent "LULU" that, if at all, Kamala Harris succeeds to the Presidency it would be "a shame on America!" "Uncle Ben" and "Cousin Cameron," Trump is actually saying after your praise of him, your daughter, sister even mother is not worthy. How do you like your apples, as pay-back?

While Black-voters value the vote they finally secured despite many obstacles, this right is becoming more challenging to express. To recall, during the Obama Administration, Attorney General Eric Holder consistently challenged Republican efforts to restrict the right to vote through the courts, state houses, propaganda pronouncements whether through radio and TV messaging, closure of polling sites across many states under their control, and requiring state issued photo identification. However, given these strategies are ongoing, now even the Post Office has come under scrutiny. As the Carona-virus pandemic continues to ravage the country, the Vote-by-Mail option seems right to encourage the American vote that strengthens the democratic process. Much of this Mr. Trump objected to and observers accused the newly appointed Postmaster General of undermining the Postal Pledge to deliver the mail, the ballots, on time to be counted.

All this notwithstanding, observers have pointed out, Blacks at the Republican National Convention seemed to speak to only one thing, Donald Trump is not a racist. They equally endorsed his claim to do more for Black-Americans than anyone since the time of Abraham Lincoln. As soon as these Blacks "Sold their brothers to the Slave dealers," they were moved from the stage while white presenters spoke about Mr. Trump's promises, those fulfilled and what to expect when he is re-elected. These Black supporters of Donald Trump, Tim Scott, but especially Dr. Ben Carson, Kentucky Attorney General Daniel Cameron, Hershel Walker, and Alice Johnson, recently released from prison after serving twenty years for a drug deal, all appeared as principals, perhaps as samples in Malcolm X's "House Negro – Field Negro" dichotomy, denying Donald Trump is a racist. That's what they were there for! Trump may have done something for any one of them as in Alice Johnson's case, but this "one Sparrow should not be summer," in vouching for Trump's every act towards Black and Brown-Americans. These apologists are thus stuck with Mr. Trump's "more baggage than Hakeem brought to America" and as new revelations expose Trump's callousness, these apologists are seen as fools whose ancestors came from "shit-hole countries."

On the other hand, and more credibly, Congresswoman Karen Bass Chairwoman of the Black Caucus, appearing on CNN's **State of the Union**, Sunday August 30, 2020, was asked by Dana Bash, sitting in for Jake Tapper, about the Black speakers who attacked Biden at the Republican National Convention, to which Ms. Bass replied:

WHO SPEAKS FOR THE BLACK VOTE IN THE AGE OF TRUMP?

1. "These individuals represented themselves," not any significant Black constituency.

2. "After 3 ½ years of Donald Trump and his administration's performance, it's shameful they could paint such a glaring portrait of someone who uttered 22,000 lies, insults everyone, is vindictive, divisive and peddles fear even towards his supporters. Let's not forget, his "shithole" degradation was repeated more than once.

3. To claim he has done more for African-Americans than anyone since Abraham Lincoln is insulting for it denies the existence of Barack Obama and Lyndon Johnson who passed the **1964 Civil Rights Act** and the **1965 Voting Rights Act** that tremendously benefitted African-Americans. Who could do more for Blacks than Barack Obama, a man of high moral principles, worked tremendously to benefit all the American people, did business white but sleeps black, possessed a tremendous work ethic and embodied the true American spirit? Contrast this with a "pathological liar," a womanizer who equally disrespects women, in love with dictators and has tremendously tarnished the American image in the eyes of the world.

4. His poor and ineffective leadership and denial of the implications of the Carona-Virus that has killed nearly 200,000 Americans, a significant percentage of whom were African-Americans is classic

dereliction of duty. He lied to the American public after confessing to Bob Woodward the Virus was five times more deadly than the flu and it was airborne, highly contagious, "and the single largest Public health failure in the US in a hundred years. According to Dana Bash, "these are unbelievable things about the virus." Dr. Peter Hotez thought it "devastating."

Now Trump is pressuring the Federal Drug Administration to "cut the vaccine foot to fit the election slipper," so he can propagandize results that are not proven to be safe and effective. Like Mr. Trump, his Blacks will deny responsibility if the rushed vaccine fails to provide the touted expectations. Elder Wisdom held, "Don't join gangs for you own their history."

Now, one "Trump's Ship of Fools," has sailed, and those trying to convince Black voters to vote for Trump despite the face he appeals to white racial resentment; denies systemic racism does not exist in America; stokes resentment and fear; paints Black as criminals as he classed Mexicans as drug dealers and rapists; or, tries to suppress the Joe Biden's challenge; **we must expose as Charlatans**! as quack who, together with Donald Trump, push untold snake oil remedies from disinfectant to convalescent plaza and more revelations, particularly the new military "losers" and "suckers" claims, in a stretch, the question then becomes, can these labels be attached to Mr. Trump's Blacks?

Quite frankly, Donald Trump has not done anything for African-Americans and does not deserve a single Black vote, except for the one who shamelessly vouched for the character despite the revered John Lewis reminding, "Donald Trump is a racist." While many determined he is narcistic, divisive, hate-filled, punitive and should not lead this great country nor be re-elected, even as more continue to unfold, shamefaced Ben Carson and DA Cameron have lost all semblance of credibility.

6. Instead of emphasizing passage of the **George Floyd Justice and Policing Act** and the **John Lewis Voting Rights Act** renewal, yet seeking to falsely portray Donald Trump as what he is not, these token blacks, Ben Carson, Daniel Cameron, shamelessly exposed themselves as hypocrites and will have to answer to the Black Community after Trump vomits them out.

Let's be clear. If Donald Trump's sister and his niece say he is a racist; then Trump's former attorney Michael Cohen, who up to the time of his legal and political troubles was considered "Mr. Trump's fixer," who "would have taken a bullet for Mr. Trump;" now Cohen says, Donald Trump is "a cheat, a liar, a fraud, a bully, a racist, a predator, a con man." Then how credible are persons as Ben Carson and DA Cameron other than shameless yes men who now own their statements, probably been paid to do so: for "What's in it for them?" Might I add, Kayleigh

McEnamy, long under scrutiny in response to Michael Cohen's book **Disloyal**: **A Memoir**, as White House Press Secretary attacked Cohen's credibility in the following statement: "Michael Cohen is a disgraced felon and disbarred lawyer, who lied to Congress. He has lost all credibility, and its unsurprising to see his latest attempt to profit off of lies." Of course, Kayleigh does not have the balls to say Mr. trump profits from his 22,000 lies! Of course, she has to disown books by John Bolton, Amarosa, D'Antonio, Bob Woodward, Max Boot, equally *Everything Trump Touches Dies*. She certainly has her work cut out for her! Thank goodness, Kelly, Mattis, Macmaster and many others have not fully told their tales as yet.

Not simply these Black apologists' credibility but Mr. Trump's has been badly damaged by the new Military thing. It's interesting to listen to two persons who served 5 presidents (former Senator Barbara Boxer) and 4 presidents (David Gergen) and whose comments are riveting. They feel disappointed by Donald Trump's actions especially in revealing the "Nuclear secret" thing.

WHO SPEAKS FOR THE BLACK VOTE IN THE AGE OF TRUMP?

The Black Vote Photo – "We will Breathe" and on the steps of the Lincoln Memorial – "Black Lives Matter."

The Black Vote Photo – "Black Lives Matter," "Vote Him Out," "Justice for All" and "Jail Killer Cops!"

The Black Vote Photo – Say their Names – Marquesha McMillan and Mary Truxillo.

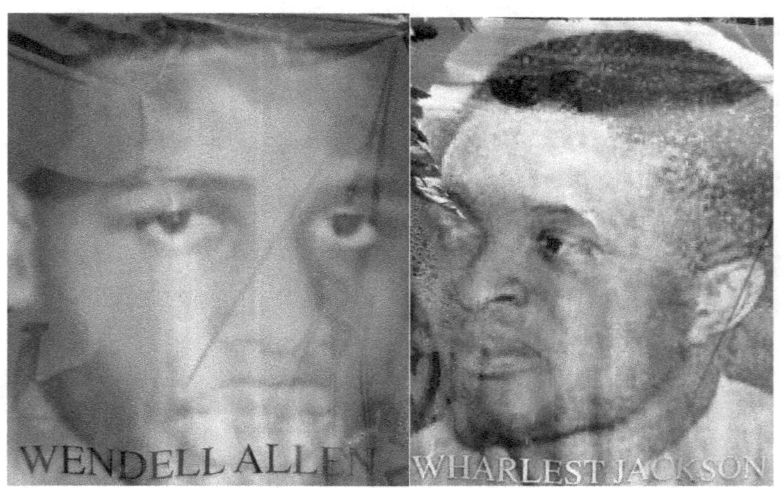

The Black Vote Photo – Say their Names – Wendell Allen and Wharlest Jackson.

WHO SPEAKS FOR THE BLACK VOTE IN THE AGE OF TRUMP?

The Black Vote Photo – "Black Live Matter" All the Time, and "With Black Power!"

The Black Vote Photo – A chain of Strong Black Men, before the Lincoln Memorial, affirming "**Black Lives Matter**" – The Family Came Out for the "March on Washington 2020."

"When growing up, I saw segregation. I saw racial discrimination. I saw those signs that said white men, colored men. White women, colored women. White waiting. And I didn't like it." **John Lewis**

"When I speak to students about the Civil Rights Movement, I say that it is impossible to stop a determined movement that is captivating the American consciousness. I think the candidacy of Sen. Obama represents the beginning of a new movement in American political history that began in the hearts and minds of the people of this nation. And I want to be on the side of the people, on the side of the spirit of history." **John Lewis**

"I think Donald Trump is dividing the American people. He is not good for America. It's not good for our standing in the rest of the world. To divide people based on race, a color, a religion, a sexual orientation, it's just ... it's just wrong." **John Lewis**

"Even in the civil rights movement, there were so many unbelievable women. They never, ever received the credit that they should have received. They did all of the, and I cannot say it, they did all of the dirty work. Hard work." **John Lewis**

The Black Vote Photo – "Malcolm X, Nelson Mandela, Huey P. Newton, Fred Hampton, Kwame Ture" and "I Can't Breathe" with the names.

27. ERIK TRUMP'S DIATRIBE BY DR. FRED MONDERSON

Sure, Erik Trump, like a dutiful son, praised his father President Donald Trump, on day two of the 2020 Republican National Convention. Commentators in post-convention analysis pointed out some misrepresentation of fact the young Trump presented in the mad Republican rush to demonize Joe Biden, his father's Democratic opponent for the Presidency, at the November 2020 election. Many of Donald's Trump's supporters, his enablers, were never concerned or publicly acknowledged for the record, as they tried to paint and portray the party leader as a far cry of whom the real Donald Trump is. Elder wisdom insisted, "If you want to know of '8' ask '9' for they live next door.

The Black Vote Photo – Images insist, "Color is not a Crime" and "Black Lives Matter."

The Black Vote Photo – Before the Lincoln Memorial, members of the Armed Forces make their presence seen, and "Black Lives Matter" as well as "Get your Knee Off Our Necks."

The Black Vote Photo – Say their Names – Matthew Burroughs and Maurice Gordon.

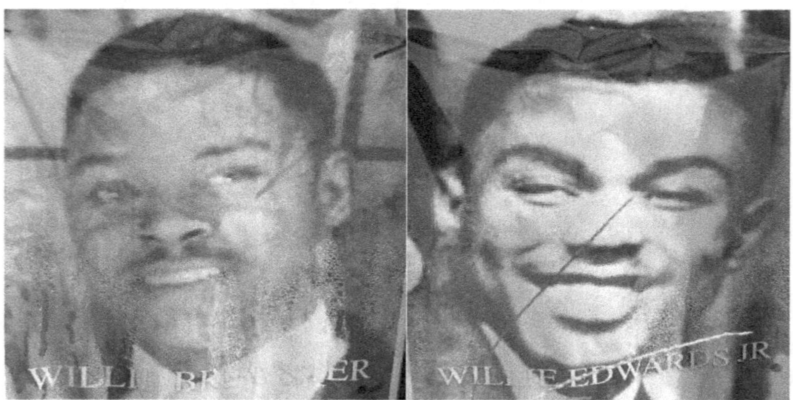

The Black Vote Photo – Say their Names – Willie Brewster and Willie Edwards Jr.

The Black Vote Photo – With the Lincoln Memorial in the background, the young men hold the Red, Black and Green with Stars, symbolic of a United Africa, then there's the Red, Black and Green!

The Black Vote Photo – "The People United Will Never be Defeated" and "Black Lives Matter!"

WHO SPEAKS FOR THE BLACK VOTE IN THE AGE OF TRUMP?

Now, if Donald Trump's sister who knew him before he was born and his niece, close family members, essentially describe him as "a dirty, rotten scoundrel," "a racist," an "anti-Semite," are we to believe three or four black men who probably received "30 pieces of silver," or as Malcolm X often determined to be "chitlings?" over these family members? As such, no matter how much powder and perfume the Trumps, Melania and the others, enablers – in and out of government lavish on President Trump, he still reeks of the "shithole" offensive odor not worthy of leading this nation and the Western Alliance. This latter is particularly significant, given Donald Trump's deference to Vladimir Putin, the alliance's principal adversary is pronounced; yet, he belabors, belittles American heroes simply because they won't agree with his outrageously objectionable behaviors.

These factors, notwithstanding, one item that stood out in Erik Trump's criticism of Joe Biden was that "He spent 47 years" in government and had nothing to show for this service. Such a warped expectation is why the "**Atlantic**" article reports American military men who died on the field of battle, given their lives to defend this nation, got nothing for their sacrifice and so are "Losers" and "Suckers."

What is interesting, about this time is that Joe Biden dedicated his life to service of the American people, their institutions and has stood for decency and the truth. Politics is such, you author some good and some bad bills but thankfully "unjust laws" can be reversed. And again, such public servants are "losers" and "suckers" However, refusal to serve when presented with the opportunity cannot later be erased. Erik's dad, on the other hand, weaseled out of national service by claiming bone spur and educational deferrals so he could "game the system" while ruthlessly building the Trump empire.

The interesting thing about Donald Trump, the narcissist; is, if anyone criticizes or says anything about him, he instantly pounces, tweets them in the most negative manner. In 2016, Michael Bloomberg, the former Mayor of New York City, called Donald Trump a "con man." In 2020, he again, at the Democratic National Convention, spoke pejoratively about Donald but his remarks were ignored. Is it because Mike Bloomberg is more than ten time richer than Trump and can be a bigger bully than he?

Poor Erik, only himself, members of the Trump family, a few testifying Blacks of little credibility, a Republican Party that shamelessly ignores Mr. Trump's 22,000 lies, fear-mongering, divisive rhetoric, poor leadership, insults, not to forget downplaying and lack of leadership that resulted in 190,000 victims of Carona-virus and so much more. Therefore, Erik can praise his father as much as he wants but he is still anything other than, "unfit to lead." He has run the American ship of state onto the rocks of near-fail-state status. His re-election may ultimately destroy a once great American nation. As a result, no self-respecting American veteran, Black voter, should vote for Donald Trump and now the people have the last laugh on men in red who, are now shamefully stuck with the "Loser" in the White House.

The Black Vote Photo – "Please don't shoot my son" and "**Black Lives Matter**."

The Black Vote Photo – People gather for the "Commitment March" and "Vote Him Out" BLM.

The Black Vote Photo – Say their Names – Medgar Evers and Megan Hockaday.

The Black Vote Photo – Say their Names – Willie McCoy and Yuvette Henderson.

The Black Vote Photo – "Ignorance allied with Power is the most ferocious Enemy Justice can Have" and "Black Excellence."

"The advent of the civil rights movement during the 50s and 60s made it very plain, crystal clear, to me that we had an obligation to do what we could to make real the Constitution of the United States of America." **John Lewis**

"As a young child, it became crystal clear to me that there were certain rights and privileges that other people had that my mother, my father, my grandparents, my great grandparents didn't have - that it was an ongoing struggle to realize the dream of the 14th and 15th Amendment." **John Lewis**

The Black Vote Photo – “No Justice, No Peace” and “Can I get a **FIST** for Black Lives Matter?”

The Black Vote Photo – “Black Lives Matter” and “BLM.”

The Black Vote Photo – GYKOT NECKS.

The Black Vote Photo – "**BLACK LIVES MATTER!**"

The Black Vote Photo – "1 man, 2 feet, 1000 miles March for Change, Justice and Equality."

The Black Vote Photo – "If you are silent about your pain, they'll kill you and say you enjoyed it" Zora Neil Hurston - and "Dr. King had a Dream 57 years ago, Where the **HELL** is my peace?"

The Black Vote Photo – "Maintain Social Distance, Wear a Mask, Use Hand Sanitizer, **PROTECT THE VOTE**!"

28. KAMALA AND MICHELLE BY DR. FRED MONDERSON

After Senator Kamala Harris noted, "When the people peacefully protested in front of the White House, Donald Trump tear gassed them" for a photo opportunity on sacred grounds of an important church. Equally too, that "American Democracy is under threat" from the President of the United States through efforts of voter suppression, under-funding and dismantling of the Post Office, even undermining the election 6-months before November 3, 2020, this is cause for concern.

Sorrowfully ignorant of election dynamics, Mr. Trump spews, "The only way the election is legitimate is if I win," is something perhaps the President of Belarus not the President of the United States, would say. Now, how in heaven's name can Donald Trump champion democracy abroad while he sabotages it at home?

On the first night of the Democratic National Convention 2020, Michelle Obama masterfully dissected and diagnosed the maladies emanating from the White House occupied by the Trump Administration that constantly spews falsity, divisive rhetoric, weak leadership, even lost in foolish aspirations of being on Mount Rushmore and being elected to a second term. In this verbal expose and condemnation, "Mighty Michelle" "Took Donald Trump to the cleaners," washed him well and hung him out to dry setting the stage for four nights of exposure of uncaring and weak leadership, the Carona-Virus failure resulting in some 190,000 American deaths, his lies, divisive rhetoric, racist rants that encourage other racists, hiding the facts, supports white racists, Q-Anon, etc., as well as his love for Putin and things Russian.

Because of the Black vote, in today's reality, Black women in leadership of major cities such as Keisha Lance Bottoms of Atlanta; Lori Lightfoot of Chicago: Muriel Bowser of Washington, DC; former Senator Carole Moseley-Braun; even the female Governor of Michigan Gretchen Michener whose service in challenging times is considered profound, reflects the role of women as voters and leaders. These women not simply speak truth to power but wield significant power in their own right, manning the fort exceptionally well. This is what Donald Trump fears from the opposite sex and especially from two Black women such as Kamala and Michelle. They bring into reality what political activists-fighters such as Fannie Lou Hamer, Queen Mother Moore, Elsie Richardson, Dorothy Height, and so many other women have contributed to the American political experience in their fight for the right to vote, and thereby garner empowerment, whether political, economic, educational and even social.

Senator Kamala Harris was chosen by former Vice-President Joe Biden to be his running mate principally because she is an incredibly competent woman who ran the second largest District Attorney and attorney General office in the nation. Ms. Harris, who, whether in questioning Justice Kavanaugh at his hearing to become a Supreme Court Jurist, and in other similar capacities brings tremendous experience to the ticket. Even more important, Senator Harris, as woman, champion, challenges the proverbial "ceiling" notion that many women have longed to shatter especially as in the case of Hillary Clinton who sought to do so in the 2016 National Election. Who could forget how Donald Trump tried to intimidate Hillary at the Debate especially him misogynistic behavior of wanting to power over her?

Observers should not underestimate Joe Biden's ability to handle bullies and it's expected he has seen and studied practically all of Donald Trump's dirty tricks. And, after 47 years in government service, plus 4 years as Vice-President, this David must have learned how to deal with crooks as Goliath.

In the movie **Rulers of Engagement**, one of the heroes said to the crooked government official, "Do you know how it feels to have a pissed off Marine on your back?" Well, Mr. Trump has challenged two of the most powerful black women in America, who are also articulate, intelligent, and have a following, black and white, who will forever champion their cause.

Then again, Mr. Trump's "barrel of troubles" has run over – Imagine:

1. Pissing off Mexicans he called drug dealers and rapists, an act he himself has been accused of in addition to sexual assault charges.

2. Accused a federal judge of Mexican heritage of not being impartial in a case of Trump against others.

3. To this day, Trump hates the name and memory of John McCain whom he called "a loser."

4. A neutered Ben Carson now praised Trump after probably being paid some "30 pieces of silver"

or given a Cabinet position he then overspent on a desk for his office and had to be reprimanded.

5. Trump thinks African nations are shit-hole countries, the place of the heritage of those who proclaimed from the Republican National Convention podium, "Donald Trump is not a racist!"

6. Trump disparages people of Black and Hispanic heritage.

7. He labels the Carona-19 Virus the "Kung Flu" and "China virus" and refuses to take responsibility for its nearly 200,000 deaths.

8. He called Amarosa "a dog."

9. Many of his opponents are "low life" and "low IQ."

10. While Mr. Trump genuflects before Vladimir Putin:

   1. He says nothing about Russian bounties on American soldiers.

   2. He disparaged American Intelligence before Putin in Helsinki.

   3. Trump vocally parroted Russian talking points on Ukraine supposed interference in the 2016 Election. Today Putin parrots mail-In-Ballot falsity first echoed by Trump.

4. He remains silent about on-going Russian interference in the 2020 election.

More to come. Still, Kamala and Michelle may be too much for Trump to handle, despite his feigned bravado. After all, their husbands are watching.

The Black Vote Photo – "I Stand with Black Women" "Power and Justice for Breonna Taylor!"

29. MICHELLE AND TRUMP BY DR. FRED MONDERSON

After Michelle Obama roasted Donald Trump on Day One of the Democratic National Convention, in the linguistically challenged manner of his continuing mannerism, the President responded, “It’s the job your husband did that enabled me to be elected.” How pathetically sad Mr. Trump could not and did not address any of the indictments leveled by Ms. Obama or the untold Republicans and democrats who spoke against either his words or thoughts, as the world listened to penetratingly exposed evidence, “this king is naked!” Thus, an interesting question for white men should be, “Is Donald Trump an ideal representative of you as a man?” That is, after he has been deemed a bigot, racist, cheat, liar, misogynist, divider, weak leader and much more. Are you then represented in the person of such an individual?

For the longest, Senator Bernie Sanders indicated, Donald Trump is a "pathological liar," but unlike his unconscionable and unrelenting attacks against anyone who criticized him, in uncharacteristic manner, Donald Trump took his Michelle flailing and moved on. No less significant, untold numbers of citizens, foreign and domestic, have expressed disgust at Mr. Trump's behavior and leadership as President of the United States and leadership of the Western Alliance. It's been pointed out, in addition to the Carona-Virus pandemic's devastation as well as Mr. Trump's treatment of America's long-standing allies, especially the fact Americans are today banned from a number of these countries in Europe as well as the well-regarded, the well-respected American passport is today valued among that of the poorest Third World nations. This is the reality of Donald Trump's America. Given the above and while great swaths of Americans across the nation protest Donald Trump's poor leadership, lack of empathy, divisive rhetoric and racism, much of this has spilled across the globe and so Donald Trump is not welcome in much of Europe, particularly.

What Mr. Trump fails to recognize and is not big enough to admit; first, not only did the stock market and the nation's entire economic infrastructure he claims and gets credit for building; was, fundamentally the work of Barack Obama. Second, no matter how he spins it, Mr. Trump and a cohort of Republican operatives, in and out of government, unrelentingly attacked the first African-American President, disrespected his person through thought, deed and vile caricature while blocking or attempting to block every legislative proposal Mr. Obama encouraged; yet still, Obama did make an imprint on the legislative agenda and in the minds and hearts of great numbers of the American people and such leadership attests to his popularity today. Interesting how, during Mr. Obama's Presidency, while his decency reflected the American persona and won praises for America abroad particularly after its image was tarnished by President Bush's "go it alone" actions in Iraq, this view has now been squandered by Donald Trump filthy persona. Nevertheless, Republicans, in their approach to President Obama painted the decent man in the most horrible manner claiming how divided he had made the nation. Talk about division, conversely while Trump's supporters, Mr. Obama's adversaries, who were ultimately exposed as racists were essentially saying was "He's not like us!" That certainly was a theme of that loser "Lipstick on a pig Sarah Palin" affirmed. Fast forward and in poor taste today, as one commentator essentially put it, "Mr. Trump's supporters recognize that their man is a liar and a dirty rotten scoundrel," but in their view, he is "'Our dirty rotten scoundrel.'" Afterall, he is loved and adored by racist, Nazis, KKK, Alt right, Q-Anon and particularly a base that kisses his dirty face and evangelicals who essentially ignored the teachings of their "Holy book!"

From the incubated "Birther" falsity and folly, through Mitch McConnell's "I intend to make Barack Obama a one-term President;" to the "Tea Party" parades in and out of government while Obama simultaneously defended their right to protest, all who coalesced into Trump supporters now simply characterized his base; but, for the most part they do not reject the dirty, rotten scoundrel appellation. Naturally, wearing blinders, these folks do not see the damage Trump has done to their nation and more important, the future of their children. The sad part, as is often said, "The children are watching" and many are being burdened with the weight of their parents' racism. Such behaviors and failure to condemn them are poisoning the future of America through their racist actions, mindset and uncaring expectation that the nation may have drifted towards a point where the damage may not be repairable.

Thus, Mr. Trump's passive response to Michelle Obama and her husband's Presidency was not only full of flaws but equally a failure to defend his own record, given the legacy Obama bequeathed him. The most significant failure in this respect has been Mr. Trump's handling of the Russian problem. Who could forget that iconic photograph of Obama meeting Putin in which the US President stared down the Russian as if to be interpreted, "I know what you are doing, attempting to do, so **STOP IT**? There is no visual image of a US attack on Russia, but in testing a new rocket, its target was an America engulfed in flames. We know Russia likes to see

WHO SPEAKS FOR THE BLACK VOTE IN THE AGE OF TRUMP?

America upended, destroyed, its institutions disrupted, division rampant among its people and any and all activities that weak this nation. Still, under President Obama, Putin and his forces feared this nation and its possible response to any overt, even covert, challenge. This is not the case with President Trump, who relished Russians in the Oval Office, and given the most recent scuttlebutt is Donald Trump is a "Russian Manchurian Candidate!" One CNN Anchor noted some 37 times when Trump and Putin interacted and not only are there no public evidence of what transpired, in all the instances Putin seemed to come out on top!

Some years ago, during his administration, *Newsweek* ran a cover story entitled, "Why are Obama's Critics so Dumb?" Today, such a cover could read, "Why are Trump's Supporters so Stupid?" Now, as this Pied Piper occupying the White House, leads his followers, particularly, into the Russian den of ovens the thought is frightening. Yet still and for example:

1. Trump's people know he is a liar, a trickster or con man, but they seem like how he shafts them and enjoys the intoxicating feeling.

2. Despite what may be said, many working for Trump have reservations about his behavior but they want to keep their jobs and so stay silent.

3. Supporters continue to ignore his failed record of leadership and the result of 190,000 Carona-Virus

deaths, a pandemic that now threatens areas in which Trump's base resides.

4. In a circular argument Mr. Trump and his supporters blame the Carona-Virus Pandemic for the nation's economic collapse, refusing to take responsibility, though this trickster who refuses to accept such responsibility took credit for the economy's rise on the foundation Barack Obama bequeathed him; yet, he disowns the downturn.

As Mr. Trump fans flames of division that encourages racial injustice he reverts to a law and order propaganda platform of panic that yet, refuses to address the underlying causes of racism that ignores social, economic, even civil and human right inequities.

5. As the nation approaches the November election, Mr. Trump began undermining the election months away. In so doing, despite safety concerns during this pandemic and particularly the efficacy of Mail-In Voting, he has railed against the same Main-In Voting and Mail-drop off measures, even as questions are raised of Post-Office failures to live up to its time proven responsibility of delivering the mail whenever.

Since his arrival, Post Master General Tom De Joy made significant and targeted changes in machinery and hourly impact on sorting and delivering the mail. Equally, this political appointee who donated to Donald Trump and Republican campaigns is now being investigated for pressuring employees to make donations to Republican candidates then reimbursing them with large bonuses and promotions in a number of ways as payback for such support. Altogether, in these and many other actions, Donald Trump has "Set a marker to dispute the election." This is significant because he has refused to say whether he will accept the results though he has said, "If I don't win, the election was not fair."

Thus, a litany of such scurrilous behaviors that characterize Donald Trump, President of the United States of America, leaves little to the imagination that exposes how America has descended to depths of indignity and how Michelle Obama was on target in calling this spade, what he is, a bigot, racist, liar, womanizer, even rapist as he was accused and an altogether poor example of a leader.

The Black Vote Photo – The Marchers say, "Black Lives Matter" and "I am a Man!"

30. THE CASE OF TWO GOVERNMENT ATTORNEYS BY DR. FRED MONDERSON

On the second day of the Republican National Convention, Kentucky Attorney General Cameron, beaming in positivity presented his view as to why Black voters especially should essentially vote to give President Trump "four more years," even as he mocked a statement Joe Biden had once said. When an individual faces the world and endorses another individual for a political office, he is essentially affirming "I'm a person of stature and chooses this person and so should you." Well, in that endorsement, the individual, such as Attorney General Cameron must own the person being endorsed.

Mr. Cameron reached back some 40-odd years into Mr. Biden's service in Congress but this lawman seems unaware of Mr. Trump's record; his objection to serve the nation in claims of having bone spurs and educational deferment, refusal to rent to Black people, calling for execution of the Central Park 5 now determined to be "The Exonerated 5" whose compensation for time served Mr. Trump objected to; the "Birther" travesty; disrespect of Black women; insult to Elijah Cummings; so much so, John Lewis exclaimed "Donald Trump is a racist;" his insensitivity to protest for as Kamala Harris eloquently stated, "When the people protested for relief in front of the White House, Donald Trump tear gassed them."

Forget the 22,000 lies, incompetent response to the Carona-Virus as told by Bob Woodward's new book, **Fear**, and Mr. Trump's call to liberate the state of Michigan especially because a woman, a democrat, was the governor. This admonition essentially encouraged and empowered vigilante and militias to take to the streets armed with long guns, many of whom appeared at the Michigan state house threatening to behead Governor Michener. That "liberate" message led militias and vigilantes into the streets of Kenosha, Wisconsin, resulting in two deaths and several wounded by one of Mr. Trump's supporters. Now, Bob Woodward's new book **Rage** mentions 18 interviews Trump gave the famous writer who essentially accuses him of "criminal negligence" for knowing the Carona Virus was 5-times more deadly than the Flu and not informing the public it was "airborne" as he continues to mislead the American people, even holding large rallies with no face coverings nor social distancing. This falsity had "a real public health effect" and could have saved more than 100,000 lives. Even more significant, when Woodward asked Trump about empathy in understanding Black-Americans' pain and anger, he responded: "I don't feel that at all! I did not drink the cool-aid" According to Chris Cuomo, he was "lying to his own supporters and their families about the dangerous Carona-virus, downplaying it and not insisting on wearing a mask and social distancing." While General Mattis thought Mr. Trump "dangerous and unfit," Woodward's take in an echo that Trump is "dangerous" and "unfit." Sorry to say, Mr. Cameron, but this and more you and the others own in your endorsement.

Given Mr. Cameron's is an elected office and to quote Rev. Al Sharpton when Kanye West made a fool of himself, before the crying incident and mental health confession, he reminded him, "Kanye, Donald Trump will not always be President and the people will remember you." The same can be applied to Mr. Cameron, especially when he seeks re-election. But then again, it's reasonable to believe he had by then received his "30 pieces of silver." Well, Mr. West flipped and he flopped and flipped again and as a barrel afloat in a storm, let this not be your lot, Mr. Cameron. Nonetheless, you own the Donald Trump lies, bigotry, divisive rantings, concealment bordering on criminality, racism, despite what you profess and thus, you are on record during "Donald Trump's time!"

The Black Vote Photo – "Wanted" and "We Will Breathe!"

In New York on the other hand, State Attorney General Tish James is investigating the Trump Organization and its significant players for all forms of illegal activities. Hopefully, because these investigations have not yet concluded, Mr. Cameron and the other Black speakers at the RNC do not own the results as yet. Nevertheless, plausible deniability in this case cannot conclude if you jumped or was pushed. In the first instance, as a lawman of any credibility you, Mr. Cameron, should especially have known better to come out and make such an outlandish statement in endorsing Mr. Trump when credible Black men such as James Clyburn, Barack

Obama, even Susan Rice and Senator Duckworth and many others determined he was rotten to the core.

The Black Vote Photo – "Enough is Enough," "I Can't Breathe" and "Black Lives Matter!"

The Black Vote Photo – "I Can't Breathe; "By Any Means Necessary;" "Erase Racism;" "Hands Up, Don't Shoot;" "No Justice, No Peace;" "Ballot or Bullets;" "Stop Killing Me;" – "Kaepernick – Strong People Stand up for Themselves; but Stronger People Stand up for Others; It takes nothing to join the Crowd, it takes everything to stand **Alone** – **Colin Kaepernick** – **You are our Hero**!"

31. PASTORS AND PASTORS BY DR. FRED MONDERSON

There was a time when the label "Man of the Cloth" had a positive meaning and the pastoral leader Pope John Paul II, among others as Rev. Herbert Daughtry, Bishop Jones, etc., best exemplified the true spirit and meaning of the appellation. In recent times, more persons have become profane essentially losing faith in what may be moral decay in drift from the high ideals of the others including Pope John Paul II's empathy and spiritual standards to the crass degradation of what was once described as "Poverty Pimps."

However, while many have sinned and come short of the glory of theology, of God, it's generally agreed most politicians go to church not particularly for spiritual salvation and rejuvenation but to be seen attending such services. In this, sin six days and seek salvation on the seventh modus operandi, politicians have inculcated and effectively utilized the church, pastors and congregations, to further their aims of being elected and reelected.

People who generally claim to not be racists are sometimes the biggest racists and Donald Trump and a significant percent of his followers fit this bill. Mr. Trump rose to political fame on the "Birther" falsity at a time when claims were being made that the nation was divided. This may very well be because Barack Obama became President and Sarah Palin expressed, "He's not like us!" Great swaths of the pastoral community remained silent as racist venom castigated Mr. Obama and it's been postulated those who pray, prayed for a savior then they "vomited out Donald Trump." Now, having made his appearance, all manner of negativity was demonstrated in his administration's nearly four years of rule. When questioned about moral depravity, one well-known pastoral leader simply responded in admitting Donald Trump's failure as a leader, certainly as a moral leader, "We have decided to give him a Mulligan!" That is to say, a form of religious, moral even social forgiveness. This is a sort of reminded of the pastoral leader Tetzel's age when he sold indulgences. However, what was not clear was whether the

Mulligan was perpetual or one time only. That is, for past sins or equally future transgression.

One of the first moves in the chess game of sinners such as Donald Trump who almost never go to church except to get a "Photo Op" after tear-gassing peaceful protesters outside the White House, is to get pastors to support their re-election bid. We know of the role Pastor Mark Burns and what's his face Darrell from Detroit played in Trump's early presidency.

A significant divide is unfolding across the pastoral landscape as black and white evangelical Christians came face to face with overwhelming evidence of racism in this country. In a recent *Washington Post* article under the heading of **Religion** entitled, "The Evangelical divide on race, social justice and Trump," by Sarah Pulliam Bailey, August 30, 2020, p. C 2, its stated: "White evangelicals angered over the killing of George Floyd this summer have joined protests and declared that 'Black Lives Matter' – and some have even championed reparations. But their continued support for President Trump has disgusted Black evangelical leaders, many of whom have let them know they are not interested."

When President Trump visited Kenosha, Wisconsin, after the shooting of James Blake he did not meet with the Black family. Instead he met with Law Enforcement personnel and when queried he stated essentially: "Sure I did not meet with the Blake family. I spoke with the Pastors." Thereafter, Mr.

Blake, Senior stated: "We don't have a pastor!" Perhaps this is another indication of Mr. Trump's shortcomings. In the interview, when a question was posed to the only Black pastor at the table, Mr. Trump cut him off and answered.

Nevertheless, let us remember, in the **House of Representatives' Impeachment Inquiry** much was made as to whether anyone close to the President had heard him say this or that and so, there was no first hand evidence that he uttered any instructions regarding issues under investigation. However, the question then becomes what is first-hand knowledge. Therefore, we look to revelations made by members of the Trump family such as his sister and niece, Mary Trump especially. Well, here's Mary take, essentially and reasons to not vote for Donald Trump, evangelical Mulligans, Black testimonials, etc., notwithstanding.

1. Donald Trump is a dangerous man.

2. He is a disgrace to our nation.

3. He uses disgusting adjectives to describe women of color.

4. Mary Trump stated, her uncle, Donald Trump is a bigot.

5. Mary Trump informed, Donald Trump is a racist and anti-Semite.

6. Mr. Trump uses language beneath the dignity of the Office of the Presidency.

7. Donald Trump is a pathological liar with some 22,000 lies or false statement to his credit.

8. His behavior is considered reprehensible.

9. Trump is on an accelerated downward spiral or as one commentator, John Harwood explained: "Mr. Trump is like a 22-Wheeler going downhill fast."

10. Many Americans express cynicism and a low-level of trust in any of Donald Trump's pronouncements.

11. When queried in regards the Post Office debacle, Donald Trump stated: "I have not spoken with the Post Master General." Later the White House confirmed they met. One wonders, perhaps they simply met and watched each other.

12. In the *Washington Post* article by Sarah Pulliam Bailey quoted above two striking comments caught the eye:

"Trump did not invent racism. Has he fueled it and poured some oil on it? Yes."

The author states further: "During the summer protests over racial justice, former NFL linebacker Emanuel Acho launched a video series called 'Uncomfortable Conversations with a Black Man;"

his first recording was viewed 11 million times on **Instagram**. The son of a Black pastor who grew up in an affluent White neighborhood and has attended predominantly White evangelical churches, Acho believes White Christians have been able to live in ignorance. “Some Christians say, ‘It’s not about race, it’s about grace. It’s not about skin, is about sin.” Even more, “It’s hard for Black people to attend predominantly White churches, specifically when White pastors are silent on the issues that matter to Black people.” And this is particularly so about the **Black Vote Especially in the Age of Trump**!

The Black Vote Photo – “Get Your Knee off Our Necks” and Black Lives Matter – I Was There!”

WHO SPEAKS FOR THE BLACK VOTE IN THE AGE OF TRUMP?

The Black Vote Photo – "The Function of Freedom is to Free Someone Else." Toni Morrison; "End Racism Now!"

The Black Vote Photo – "Maya, WEB, Spike, Frederick, Madam C J, Martin, Thurgood, Garvey, Obama – Dream, Inspire, Educate, Speak, Build.

The "Black Vote Photo – "Killing Should Not be a First Option" and "We Will!"

The Black Vote Photo – "Black + Millennial = Cultural Icon" and "Black Lives Matter Because .."

The Black Vote Photo – "Black Lives Matter" – "Black Lives Matter – Say their Names."

The Black Vote Photo – "Mood" and "Black Lives Matter" – "Justice for All!"

The Black Vote Photo – "Restore Voting Rights."

www.ingramcontent.com/pod-product-compliance
Lightning Source LLC
Chambersburg PA
CBHW060041100426
42742CB00014B/2653

* 9 7 8 1 6 1 0 2 3 0 6 9 8 *